THE

GREAT BRAIN

ROBBERY

Acknowledgments

The authors would like to thank Judith
and Averil for their unflagging support
and counsel. We also wish to record
our gratitude to Gil Simpson from
Cardinal Network and Christopher
Paulsen of House of Travel Holdings,
who assisted with the overseas travel
incurred researching this book.
Dr Keith Cameron was never too busy
to take our calls, and helped us make
sense of reams of research. Likewise,
Dr Stephen Grice graciously allowed
us to frequently interrupt him at work.
And Shaun Scott who was a patient
provider of computer advice.

Without the encouragement, advice
and material assistance of David Wale
and John Beattie, this book would
never have got off the starting blocks.
It was Sally Harding who guided it
into the home straight and across the
finishing line, with editing help from
Denis Welch. The photographs were
taken by Melanie Burford, Simon
Forsyth and Georg Ludwig. Inspector
Grant O'Fee of the Porirua Police
provided additional material.

We also wish to thank Lesley, Joseph,
Anne, Bart and Jeremy for telling us the
personal stories that form part of this
book. All the stories are true, but some
of the names and photographs have
been altered to protect families who
are still grieving.

Thank you to Communication Arts
Limited and Simon & Associates
for their generous assistance in
the creation of this document.

The trainer was giving last-minute instructions
to the jockey and appeared to slip something into
the horse's mouth just as a steward passed by.
'What was that?' inquired the steward.
'Oh, nothing,' said the trainer, 'just a minty.'

He offered one to the steward.
'Here have one. And I'll have one myself.'

After the suspicious steward left, the trainer
continued his riding instructions.
'Just keep the horse on the rails, son. You're on a
certainty. The only thing that could possibly pass
you down the straight is either the steward or me.'

THE

GREAT BRAIN

ROBBERY

Tom Scott, Trevor Grice

AURUM PRESS

First published in Great Britain
1998 by Aurum Press Ltd
25 Bedford Avenue, London WC1B 3AT

First published 1996
The Publishing Trust
PO Box 1407
Wellington
New Zealand

A catalogue record for this book is available from the British Library.

ISBN 1 85410 569 8

10 9 8 7 6 5 4 3 2 1
2002 2001 2000 1999 1998

Printed and bound in Great Britain by
Butler & Tanner Ltd, Frome

CONTENTS

INTRODUCTION
Why we wrote this book

Part 1 - The Challenge

This section covers the problems that parents and their teenage children are likely to encounter when the question of drug use arises – particularly with marijuana. We explain in simple terms how the brain works and give space to ordinary people who have consented to tell their own stories about the hazards and tragedies of drug use.

CHAPTER 1   PUBERTY BLUES   13
The stresses and strains of adolescence

CHAPTER 2   IS MY CHILD ON DRUGS?   15
How to spot the warning signs

CHAPTER 3   A MOTHER'S STORY   21
The waste of a life

CHAPTER 4   HOW THE BRAIN WORKS   25
The most advanced computer on earth

CHAPTER 5   VANDALISM IN THE REFINERY   29
What drugs can do to the brain

CHAPTER 6   YOU MUST REMEMBER THIS   33
Drugs and memory loss

CHAPTER 7   WHAT IS MARIJUANA?   37
The facts about cannabis

CHAPTER 8   THE STORY OF TWO USERS   43
'We knew we were sick'

CHAPTER 9   SO WHO'D BE A PARENT?   47
When kids push the limits

CHAPTER 10   WHAT CAN WE DO?   49
Don't just sit there, make a list

CHAPTER 11   KIDS, THIS IS FOR YOU   54
20 ways to say no to drugs

CHAPTER 12   A SISTER'S STORY   57
A sibling slays the dragon

CHAPTER 13   GETTING OFF DRUGS   60
Only you can choose

CHAPTER 14   A COUNSELLOR'S STORY   62
The three-month challenge

CHAPTER 15   CONCLUSION   65

CONTENTS

Part 2 - The Danger List

This section provides itemised information about all the most common drugs from alcohol to heroin. This section, which is in alphabetical order, can be used as a ready-reference guide to the origins, ingredients, effects and dangers of drugs.

CHAPTER 16	ALCOHOL	68
CHAPTER 17	AMPHETAMINES	72
CHAPTER 18	BARBITURATES	74
CHAPTER 19	CAFFEINE	78
CHAPTER 20	COCAINE	80
CHAPTER 21	HALLUCINOGENS	84
CHAPTER 22	INHALANTS	90
CHAPTER 23	MARIJUANA	92
CHAPTER 24	NICOTINE	98
CHAPTER 25	OPIATES/NARCOTICS	100
CHAPTER 26	STEROIDS	104

Part 3 - The Hard Science

This section explains in more detail how nerve impulses are generated, transmitted and interfered with in the brain.   106

USEFUL ORGANISATIONS	112
GLOSSARY	112
INDEX	117

Possession
isn't nine-tenths
of the law,
it's nine-tenths
of the problem.

John Lennon

INTRODUCTION

WHY WE WROTE THIS BOOK

I am a child of the 60s. I went to Massey University at the height of Flower Power and flatted in a series of dilapidated old houses in Palmerston North.

Tom Scott

In one flat I painted a giant mural of Jimi Hendrix on one wall and the chemical formula of LSD in special paint on another. The formula glowed with a ghostly luminescence under the fluorescent light we were very proud of. It was at a party where 'A Day in the Life' from Sgt Pepper was being played over and over that I saw my first joint being passed around.

Not being a smoker I couldn't suck on burning vegetable matter without my throat hurting or my eyes watering copiously. I was having enough difficulty impressing girls as it was, so I decided it would seem hipper to refuse than to double over coughing and spluttering. I didn't indulge then, and don't now, but I defended other people's right to.

When my own children reached the age when indulging became a possibility, I began to re-examine my position. Other teenagers who smoked marijuana regularly – children of my friends and friends of my children – were dropping out of school and getting into trouble. It was then that I began to suspect that marijuana wasn't quite as benign as was commonly assumed.

This suggestion is anathema to many of my contemporaries and colleagues in the media. Cannabis (the plant from which marijuana comes) has enjoyed a good press from my generation – the ruling wisdom being that if getting stoned wasn't exactly good for you, it did you little harm either, and in the process you had a nice time and – if you were really lucky – received insights into the mysteries of the cosmos.

Historically, the case against marijuana has relied more on anecdotal evidence than on hard data. The 'reefer madness' foaming at the mouth, anti-marijuana propaganda films of the 40s didn't exactly help the debate. Authoritative drug research is costly and time-consuming, and in the past the various disciplines involved have tended to work in isolation, with the result that their findings have been piecemeal and sometimes contradictory.

Some social scientists, self-appointed experts and assorted lobbyists call for more lenient attitudes to cannabis use, on the grounds that it is 'less harmful than alcohol' and that marijuana is an exception to the rule that recreational drugs have toxic side effects. This mantra, echoed by an often gullible media, has drowned out the polite demurrings of research chemists, toxicologists, neurophysiologists and clinicians.

Indeed, up until recently it was possible to defend cannabis on the grounds that the jury was still out. Not any longer. Scientists from around the world have filed back into the courtroom, and the verdict is guilty.

This book had its origins in the desire to bring that guilty verdict to the attention of parents, teachers and kids, but somewhere along the way it grew in size and scope to include all the drugs of abuse (see reference section at back). I don't know how I agreed to that, I must have been on something pretty strong at the time. The small six-month project Trevor Grice promised me wound up consuming the best part of three years.

Where the science makes sense and meaning soars into flight, Trevor and I pay homage to the wonderful men and women who work long unglamorous hours in laboratories on behalf of all of us. Where the facts seem leaden-footed and the information refuses to dance, the blame is Trevor's alone.

Tom Scott
Kilbirnie, Wellington

Mortuaries are the hidden places of society, the dust under the rug of our communities, especially when the deceased are lying there not of natural causes but of suicide or misadventure.

I remember vividly my first visit to one: I stood

Trevor Grice

there looking down on this youthful distorted face, a mere boy of some scholastic ability who had been tipped to be a high achiever. The warder had pulled him on the trolley into better light, a cardboard tag was tied to his big toe. His face was frighteningly discoloured, as it had been some days since they found him. No words transpired, just a nod of my head, a signature, and later facing his distressed parents, the inevitable coroner's report, the funeral, grief and memories.

Over the next 25 years, because of the nature of my work, I was to identify dozens of young people with similar endings. Frustration, despair and anger would manifest itself, especially when you knew it all started with drug experimentation, then regular use, then regular abuse, and from lesser drugs to greater drugs, and from lesser amounts to greater amounts.

The tragedy of drug use with children and adolescents is that they absorb these substances much faster than adults, the blood level of these drugs will consequently be higher and their effect on the body greater. Their livers metabolise them (break them down into smaller compounds) less

THIS CANNABIS EDUCATION RESOURCE BOOKLET WILL HELP TEACHERS HELP PUPILS WORK OUT WHAT LEVEL OF BRAIN DAMAGE IS RIGHT FOR THEM...

efficiently, and their kidneys excrete them (eliminate them from the body) more slowly. At the same time their personality, intellect, and body systems are undergoing profound changes thus rendering them vastly more susceptible to harm than adults, who, in theory anyway, are fully formed and mature.

I hope that this book will empower parents and will help teenagers to delay any decisions about drug use until they have completed maturation. The process of maturation can last seven years from the onset of the first signs.

I have taken considerable inspiration from Pablo Casals, who said:

'Sometimes I look about me with a feeling of complete dismay. In the confusion that afflicts the world today, I see a disrespect for the very values of life. Beauty is all around us, but how many are blind to it! They look at the wonder of this earth and seem to see nothing.

'Each second we live is a new and unique moment of the Universe, a moment that will never be again...

'And what do we teach our children? We teach them that two and two make four and that Paris is the capital of France.

'When will we also teach them: Do you know what you are? You are a marvel. You are unique. In all the years that have passed, there has never been another child like you. And look at your body – what a wonder it is. Your legs, your arms, your fingers, the way you move. You may become a Shakespeare, a Michelangelo, a Beethoven. You have the capacity for anything. Yes, you are a marvel. And when you grow up, can you then harm another who is, like you, a marvel? You must cherish one another. You must work – we all must work – to make this world worthy of its children.'

We accept that people take mood-altering substances, because they enjoy altering their moods. But there is a low for every high. A return journey for every trip. What every child entering adolescence needs to understand is that there is no short cut to happiness through chemistry. There is just a short circuit of the unique brain wiring that makes them, them.

Trevor Grice
Tararua Ranges

PART 1

··

THE CHALLENGE

PUBERTY BLUES

THE STRESSES AND STRAINS OF ADOLESCENCE

In a perfect world all adolescents would start puberty at the same time – the beginning of the school year would be nice. Puberty would be of fixed duration and all the physical and psychological changes would be synchronised. Adolescence would then be a well-defined, finite, predictable business.
It isn't.

The physiology of adolescence may be the same the world over, but psychologically the path to adulthood has different lengths in different cultures. In the Third World it can be traversed in an afternoon. In the West, if you are a typically impatient teenager, it can seem like an eternity.

Some boys get pimples and sprout hair alarmingly all over their top lip, yet stubbornly remain the same height for ages. They wake up one morning and their voice has dropped, and something else has dropped as well. Some girls sprout hair alarmingly from other regions of their bodies and grow eight inches in eight months, yet spend hours staring anxiously into empty bra cups waiting for things to happen.

Everyone goes through puberty in their own messy, magical way. One of the great wonders of life is that we are all utterly unique. Each of us is constructed from our own special blueprint (our chromosomes), and on that master-plan quite distinct parental, cultural, religious and social influences are imprinted.

The onset of puberty is not always easy to spot. Some of the clues are very subtle. A useful signal, however, is the overwhelming urge to look up words like COITUS, GONADS and ORGASM in the dictionary. Children find these definitions easy to locate, as most school dictionaries spring open automatically at the required pages – probably because 25 years earlier their parents were looking up the same words.

Adolescence: a stage between infancy and adultery.

H. L. Mencken

Curiosity about COITUS, GONADS and ORGASM is one of the early indications that the brain is preparing the body to abandon childhood.

It does this by running a tape measure over the rest of the body, and if all the systems are ready it instructs the pituitary (a special gland at the base of the brain just above the roof of the mouth) to unleash hormones (chemical messengers) that travel in the bloodstream to the gonads (testicles in boys, ovaries in girls) and tell them to start producing sex hormones (testosterone in boys, oestrogen and progesterone in girls).

At this point, all hell breaks loose. Physically, mentally, emotionally and spiritually they will never be the same again.

And the single most common factor for all adolescents moving through this potentially explosive process is stress.

A father is a banker provided by Nature.

Oxford Book of Aphorisms

◆ **THE STRESS IS PHYSICAL**

Growing extra bone and muscle and beginning to ovulate or produce spermatozoa is a time-consuming, energy-sapping business. Adolescents, like infants, require more sleep in order to recharge the body's electro-chemical systems.

◆ **THE STRESS IS EMOTIONAL**

These startling physical changes, arriving without warning, often cause confusion, disorientation, guilt and panic in the unprepared.

◆ **THE STRESS IS MENTAL**

At the very time their testicles are letting them know they are there, these would-be adults are expected to solve complicated algebra problems and remember the annual rainfall of the Amazon basin. Their breasts throb with pain, yet they are supposed to go into raptures over Shakespeare's sonnets and understand photosynthesis too. Parents and teachers are exhorting them to settle down and concentrate while the rest of their world is topsy-turvy.

Academic pressure from the front of the classroom and at home doesn't always seem that relevant when right alongside you other pupils are changing in all sort of ways – loyalties shift and jealousies emerge as old friends make new friends and you may be left out.

To mature at a different rate is to fall out of step with your contemporaries. Anyone falling behind is open to feelings of abandonment and ridicule. 'Nerds' fall behind and are targets for bullying. On the other hand, anyone getting ahead can feel awkward and embarrassed. Finding old friends immature, they are suddenly open to the charge of being 'stuck up'.

Ahead, behind or perfectly in step, every adolescent in their search for a comfortable identity fears teasing and rejection, has difficulty communicating emotions and can at times feel terribly powerless.

If that weren't bad enough, when children reach adolescence, many parents change for the worse. Overnight they become boring, selfish, insensitive, impatient, intolerant, ignorant, penny-pinching, nagging, suspicious, paranoid, dogmatic, judgmental, vindictive, sneaky, calculating, obsessed with hygiene, obsessed with order, obsessed with possessions, hyper-irritable, hyper-critical, hyper-anxious, over-protective, humourless, conservative, and deeply embarrassing to their children and their children's friends.

Mercifully these symptoms tend to disappear when adolescents complete maturation and move into their late teens. Most parents have fully recovered by the time their children reach their 20s.

IS MY CHILD ON DRUGS?

HOW TO SPOT THE WARNING SIGNS

Given all the tensions and frustrations of adolescence, imagine how a teenager might feel on being handed a substance that when inhaled, ingested or injected is said to make all your hassles vanish. The temptation to experiment is understandably considerable.

So are the risks.

All teenagers are difficult, withdrawn, secretive and utterly self-centred at least some of the time. Teenagers with drug problems are difficult, withdrawn, secretive and utterly self-centred most of the time.

Parents worried about which category their teenager might belong in should rely on their instincts. All parents want to be able to trust their children but that shouldn't mean ceasing to trust your own intuition. Almost without exception, no one knows a child better than its own parents, and almost without exception no one cares about that child more than its own parents.

Of course, children and adolescents using drugs seldom announce this fact to their parents. When asked directly if they are using drugs they will probably deny it angrily or scoff loudly at the mere suggestion. For the sake of a quiet life kids know it's easier to lie to their parents, and for the sake of a quiet life many parents – intuition notwithstanding – are tempted to believe them. Denial is not confined to drug users alone – many parents will go to extraordinary lengths to blind themselves to the obvious.

For some parents the moment of truth is forced on them. Their children's lies collapse of their own accord or there is a knock on the door from the authorities. There is no need, however, to wait nervously for that knock on the door confirming your worst fears – if you know what to look for, even the most secretive and calculating child on drugs will unwittingly provide all the corroborative evidence needed to establish the truth.

The clues range from changes in behaviour to changes in physical appearance. Some of these signs can indicate other medical conditions, but a combination of the ones listed below, especially if they are of recent occurrence, should raise serious questions in parents' minds. Adolescents worried about a brother, sister or friend should look for the same telltale signs.

BEHAVIOURAL CHANGES

♦ Dramatic and unexpected changes in attitude.

♦ Isolation in room for unusual lengths of time.

♦ Habitual lying; will cover one lie with another.

♦ Tardy, delinquent behaviour.

♦ Violence, physical and/or verbal.

♦ Secretive behaviour, such as sneaking away and making excuses about where they are going or where they have been.

♦ Strange and secretive telephone calls.

♦ Shoplifting and stealing; unexplained disappearance of money or valuables (e.g., CDs that can be sold easily) from the family home or friends' homes.

♦ Disregard and disrespect for the values of the home and indifference to other members of the family.

♦ Manipulates parents one against the other.

♦ Wears sunglasses at inappropriate times.

SCHOOL-RELATED CHANGES

♦ Sudden or gradual drop in school grades and achievement levels.

♦ Working well below their level of ability.

♦ Disrespect, defiance towards teachers, rules and regulations.

♦ Being inattentive in class; difficulty with studying.

♦ Skipping classes, frequent truancy, suspensions.

PHYSICAL CHANGES

♦ Erratic sleeping and eating habits.

♦ Dramatic weight changes, beyond normal weight loss or gain.

♦ Slurred speech.

♦ Burns on hands or clothing.

♦ Constant sniffing, runny eyes and nose; difficulty fighting off colds and infections.

MENTAL AND EMOTIONAL CHANGES

♦ Emotional outbursts, rapid mood swings.

♦ Vagueness about company kept and where time was spent.

♦ Distorted time sense.

♦ Loss of short-term memory.

♦ Shorter attention span.

♦ Exaggerated sensitivity to self; insensitivity to others.

♦ Difficulty concentrating on a single task.

♦ Unreasonable resentments.

SOCIAL CHANGES

♦ Changes in peer group, with little interest in old friends.

♦ Trouble with authority figures and the law.

♦ Seems to have money, but no job.

♦ Has job, but always needs more money.

As for more concrete evidence, alarm bells should definitely ring in your head if you happen to find – usually clumsily hidden – any of the following in your teenager's room: pipes, bongs, plastic bags, rolling papers, seeds, stems, razor blades, mirrors, blackened spoons and knives, small tins, a portable heat source such as a primus, a strange smoky smell in clothing or any other indicators of drug paraphernalia.

And if everything else fails, and suspicion still remains...

TRY THIS SIMPLE TEST:

Devised by a Californian research scientist and treatment specialist, Dr Forrest Tennant, this is a very simple test for suspected teenage marijuana abuse. There are no laboratory tests involved and you can do this in the privacy of your own home.

(By the way, don't let some of the chemical terminology bother you. We're getting to that stuff shortly. Just see if the memory problems sound familiar.)

Here's how Dr Tennant explains the Tennant test:

'If I've got a teenager in my office and I think they're using marijuana, I say, "I want you to tell me what time you got up yesterday morning."

'I have them give me the time. Then I ask them, "What did you do when you got up? What clothes did you put on? What did you eat for breakfast? What time did you go to school? What did you study in school? What did you watch on TV?" I make them go hour by hour through the day before. If they've lost their acetylcholine they don't know – they can't remember.

'They'll give you the biggest song and dance you ever heard. "Well, I, you know…I got up. I know I got to school…and I watched TV… and I just hung out." They'll give you all these vague terms just like an Alzheimer's case. They'll avoid the question.

'Now think about it for just about 10 seconds. You can remember what time you got up yesterday morning. You can probably remember what clothes you put on, what you ate for breakfast, and when you went to work, and what you ate for lunch, and where you went after work, and what you did last night.

'It's not that tough. And just remember, if you can do it, teenagers sure as heck ought to be able to. And if they can't do it, what you've just diagnosed, and what you don't need blood tests to confirm, is acetylcholine deficiency. And that's somebody getting into trouble with marijuana. If they're losing their memory, you've got a big problem in a teenager.

'It's a simple test that doesn't cost any money and is particularly relevant for teenagers, because their reservoirs of neurochemicals are more fragile than adults', and so are their brain receptor sites. They are much more susceptible than adults to probable dependence and damage.'

Children and adolescents who fit the above warning signs or fail the Tennant test almost certainly have a problem with substance abuse. But proving that someone has a problem and getting them to do something about it are two different things. It could also be a problem they are not ready to acknowledge – they may argue that their drug-taking is harmless, or that they know the risks and are operating well within what they consider their safety margins.

Forcing people to change their behaviour against their will is ethically questionable and therapeutically dubious. The best solutions to substance abuse problems come when people openly accept they have a problem and choose of their own accord to change their behaviour, which may or may not involve the help and support of others.

This can and does happen - see, for instance, Chapter 8 ('The Story of Two Users', page 41) - and it's proof that self-preservation is a powerful drive in all of us. Even the most zealous anarchist, dedicated to the complete overthrow of the state, drives home from meetings on the correct side of the road. The only people who willingly leap off tall buildings are those who know that the practice is harmful to their health.

But anyone struggling to accept that they have a substance abuse problem would be immeasurably helped if they had some understanding of how their brain

was currently operating, compared with how it used to perform.

Even though we all carry one round in our heads, most of us have scarcely begun to grasp what an incredibly complex, wonderfully responsive, yet terribly fragile instrument the brain is. Every brain is a miraculous tapestry utterly unique to the weaver – and there are no huge looms capable of manufacturing exact replicas. When

He who is convinced against his will is of the same opinion still.

Proverb

we tear that tapestry we are
damaging a one-off that can't be
easily – perhaps never – mended.

In the following chapters we
take a closer look at just how the
brain works – and the
damage that can so
easily be done to it.
But first, a
mother's story.

A MOTHER'S STORY

THE WASTE OF A LIFE

It is just over a year since Emily's death, and the pain is only starting to lift. I had 15 good years with her and three bad ones. I am left with a feeling of futility at the waste of an intelligent, beautiful and artistic little girl's life. I will never see Emily exhibit her art. I'll never see her be a bridesmaid at her sister's wedding, or be a bride herself. I will never hold the grandchildren she would have given me. When I am an old lady she will not be there to hold my hand when I die.

It all started with the beatings at high school. She was still very little and the big kids picked on her. Not that she was blameless – she told me she liked winding people up. The final straw was when she had her nose punched down at the mall by one of the group.

The police were called, and at a family group conference the girl concerned apologised. We thought it was all sorted and we could relax, but by the start of the new school year Emily's behaviour had deteriorated and she became a very different person – telling lies, disobeying all our rules and having big mood swings. Her father and I felt frightened and hopeless. Her new friends were the 'bad kids' at school and she said she now felt popular.

I asked Social Services for help, but they could only offer me a family group conference in six weeks' time. Our next step was to get an appointment with a psychologist for the whole family, as the whole family was on the receiving end of Emily's behaviour.

> I found being frightened was a normal everyday feeling.

That was a big mistake. She only came to one of the four appointments and then she stared at the ceiling the whole time and wouldn't participate at all. Then we discovered 'tough love' and we felt more in control, even though Emily called us 'Mr and Mrs Hitler'.

Then the bomb dropped – the school was suspending her for drinking on the school raffle-selling day. The headmaster told me they suspected her of dope smoking. That would have certainly explained some of her behaviour and her deteriorating school work. She was overjoyed to be rid of her 'dumb school' and went around home laughing. We were all very upset and cried heaps, which made Emily laugh even more. I felt frightened of Emily, something I never thought possible.

The school phoned me to let me know she could come back if she attended counselling, but by this time Emily had run away with her friend Janice. The police were informed she was missing and we spent the next 10 days looking for her. Her friends moved her from place to place, to keep one step ahead of us. When she turned up at home she was dirty, smelly, exhausted, very angry and defiant.

School was due to start again, and as her last school wouldn't have her back, I tried the other two high schools near us. But because she was suspected of smoking dope, neither would have her.

One school said they would take her if she agreed to regular drug testing – she refused, of course. I was dreading having her hanging around home, as she had been

threatening me with violence. I asked a family friend for help. He was associated with a church group that had a girls' hostel, and they took Emily in. She was enrolled at Linwood High School and we were able to settle down a bit ourselves.

Within a short time, though, the same cycle of bad behaviour and dope-using started again with her new schoolfriends. My weight by this time had plummeted to seven stone. She started running away again and got taken in by the St Alban's parish and placed with a young couple of schoolteachers. I started to pick up but it was too good to be true: she started playing up and was asked to leave. She sat her School Cert and got A and B marks. At the end of the year Harry's brother in Auckland invited Emily to go with his family for a North Island tour for four weeks, so off she went.

When she came home she was just like her old self. She enrolled at Hagley High School in five subjects as a sixth-former, even though she was only 15. Her father built her a room of her own. It had new carpet and red velvet curtains chosen by

her. But within a few weeks the bad behaviour started again and Social Services were as useless as before. The school counsellor made appointments for us all which we attended but Emily did not.

Emily ran away again several times. With all the money I'd spent on her room, I felt robbed and angry. We reported her missing to the police. After two weeks and a lot of detective work by me, I located her staying with an ex-schoolfriend's family in Redcliffs – she had told them 'Mum' had said she could leave home.

I tried to persuade her to come back home but Social Services wouldn't back me. She got a part-time job to pay her way, and moved out of that house to live in a flat with her yucky boyfriend. The landlord gave me the creeps. He said he would keep a fatherly eye on her.

By that time she was 16 and able to apply for the independent youth benefit without our consent. We went with her to the interview anyway. The officer was really young, and despite me telling her about Emily's drug-taking she backed Emily. I felt angry and

Her death was such a small mistake.

EMILY VANESSA BROWN
28·3·1975   11·12·1993
Treasured daughter of
HAROLD & LESLEY BROWN
Special little sis of
SELENA & ROBERT
YOU CAME INTO OUR LIVES AND
LEFT FOOT PRINTS ON OUR HEARTS
Always our Em

helpless. We didn't seem to count. I knew then I had lost all hope of any control. On the way out Emily said, 'I'll chuck in my job so I can lie in bed all day.'

The landlord kicked her boyfriend out and started supplying her with dope and making passes at her. She left there quickly and ended up in a central city flat that was only fit to be condemned. There was dirt piled up against the walls, there were no floor coverings, everyone slept on mattresses on the floor, and no dishes were ever done. It only cost $40 a week, so there was plenty left over for drugs and alcohol.

She really hit it hard in that flat. Her clothes were dirty too. My beautiful daughter had lost all her soft pretty looks.

I tried Social Services and the police again, but had no luck. Her father and I talked to her for the millionth time. Her friends were harder, older addicts. Every night without fail I was awake worrying about her and wondering if there was anything I could do to bring this nightmare to an end.

Often when I visited her she was intoxicated and abusive. The house was freezing in the winter and she slept in her clothes. She asked to come home, so I collected her quickly and brought her and her smelly clothes here. Most of her underwear went into the rubbish tin on the end of a stick. As I wouldn't let her boyfriend doss down in the spare room with her, she got angry and went back to the grotty house. She left on Thursday. On Saturday she rang to say the house had burned down at 10 o'clock that morning and she had escaped by climbing out of a window.

I felt relieved that she was alive and hoped that the bad fright would make her think. She came home and was well-behaved, but was gone again in two weeks.

A series of yucky flats followed, with equally awful people. One house had a large supply of dope growing in the back yard, which I reported to the police, but there was no action taken.

I think it was at that house that she started using prescription pills and/or needles. The deterioration was marked. I challenged her to get into rehab, as did her straight friends. I found being frightened was a normal everyday feeling. She lived for six months with a boy who had been an addict for years and been in prison several times.

I only went there if asked. They were filthy and so were their clothes, they hardly ate and the dog pooed inside. I increased my visits for the sole purpose of picking up and listing the empty pill bottles lying everywhere. One particular city doctor was involved. I submitted the list to the drug squad, they referred me to the Ministry of Health, and I then made an official complaint. I found another example of one law for doctors and another law for us.

Her health was suffering now and I had no doubt that she was going to die. She came home to us for two weeks, and every day she would disappear for a while – to use, I supposed. She was cleanly clothed and had a clean bed, and she would say, 'Mum, I love you helping me be clean here. It feels so nice' – but soon she was gone to another awful flat, with three men who used drugs.

One day when they were out, the house was firebombed. Emily was really scared and put herself into a church home and started going to Narcotics Anonymous meetings. I felt she had turned a corner and I felt good for the first time in years, but late at night two weeks later she rang to say she was moving on and going to live with her mates, and I was in the depths of despair again.

I didn't hear from her for four weeks – she said she was in a nice clean house, and when she came to see us one lunchtime she was looking the best I had seen her for ages, and my hopes were up again.

The next day when I was sitting on the toilet, I had a visualisation of her death notice in the paper. I told myself that 99 percent of the bad things that we think will happen don't eventuate.

On Saturday 11 December 1993, I arrived back from collecting a newspaper and the police car was at the gate. As the policeman came towards me I just knew. I said, 'She is dead, isn't she?'

Even though I was partially prepared, the pain and grief was just as big. Her death was such a small mistake, her drug patches fell off at a rock concert and instead of going straight home to put on new ones she bought an addict's one-day supply of methadone, then when she got home she put her patches on, and the effect was to overdose her at about 6.00 am in her sleep.

Our Maori friends helped us and we had Emily at home for people to visit, and many, many people came. It was really great to be able to talk to her about anything without her answering back, and now I knew she was 100 percent drug-free and would never use again. We buried her in Prebbleton country cemetery, next to her grandmother.

– Lesley

HOW THE BRAIN WORKS

THE MOST ADVANCED COMPUTER ON EARTH

Nature is ruthlessly efficient and economical. There is no wasted effort: if human beings have two kidneys, it's because they don't need three. Similarly, nature goes to the considerable trouble of housing the heart and lungs in a cage of rib and muscle because it deems those organs vital and worthy of protection.

Nature goes even further with the brain, housing it in an imposing fortress, a castle of bone atop a lofty vantage point with good views over the rest of the body and its surrounding terrain. Inside this fortress is 1.5 kg of jelly the size of a grapefruit, and wrinkled on the outside like an overgrown walnut. This unspectacular pinky-grey organ is quite possibly the most wondrous creation in the universe.

The brain consists of two kinds of cell: glia and neurons. Glial cells are about 10 times more numerous but only about a tenth of the size and so take up much the same space as neurons. Apart from supplying nutrients to the neurons and helping to dispose of wastes, the glial cells act as ballast – much like the polystyrene bubble packing that surrounds sensitive electronic equipment when you buy it new.

Neurons are the nerve cells that carry impulses (tiny electrical messages). These are the ones that basically do the mental business – and there are at least 100 billion of them, all capable of making as many as 10,000 connections each. There could be as many as 100 trillion connections in a single brain. More 'bits' than any computer yet dreamed of.

It has been estimated that were we able to build a computer of this complexity and sophistication it would have to be housed in a building 80 storeys high and cover an area the size of Texas. Even assuming there was enough hydro-electricity in the United States and Canada to

> If the brain was so simple we could understand it, we would be so simple that we couldn't.
>
> *Lyall Watson*

So far, the most advanced computer on earth can't duplicate a four-year-old's language ability. It can't even build a bird's nest.

Judith Hooper & Dick Teresi
The 3-Pound Universe

run such a machine it might still be no smarter than your average cocker spaniel.

The 100 billion neurons that make up the hardware in the human brain took over a million years to evolve. 100 billion neurons at birth still only leaves you with a stone-age brain. But this stone-age brain, when exposed to the twentieth century, rapidly matures into a twentieth-century brain.

Other organs mature by growing in size – under instruction from the brain. There is no difference between an adult's heart and an infant's heart – the former is merely a larger version of the latter. It is the same for bone and muscle. However an adult's brain is markedly more complicated than its infant version.

There is a comparable number of neurons but there are vastly more connections. Many of the most important connections are made during maturation (the process of shifting from childhood into young adulthood).

In order to hold a single thought for just a fraction of a second, millions of neurons have to simultaneously connect. They make contact with each other through projections called axons – which meet but don't quite touch. (See Hard Science, page 103.) The tiny gap separating each neuron from its neighbour is called a synapse. Information is carried down the axons electrically and across synapses chemically. These chemicals are

A hundred billion neurons, a hundred trillion connections – that's more than enough to contain a soul.

Judith Hooper, Dick Teresi
The 3-Pound Universe

called neurotransmitters. This place where electricity and chemistry meet is the site of drug action.

Put it another way. Electrical impulses in the brain are like runners in a 4 x 400 relay – they cover long distances at great speed. Neurotransmitters are like the batons exchanged between the runners. Our brains exchange 'batons' when transmitting the signals needed to process information, regulate emotions and keep us alive. Neurotransmitters make us think, feel and act. Drug taking quite literally has heavy users dropping the baton and pulling out of the race.

When neuroscience was in its infancy it was assumed that there was only one neurotransmitter. Over the next 50 years dozens more were discovered – and in the past five years a new one seems to have been discovered every month. Some scientists predict that there could be more than 2000 of them in the brain.

Neuroscience would be a lot simpler if God had settled for just two neurotransmitters. By the same token, a piano with only two keys would be easier to play, but it would not be capable of the infinite variety of melodies available from a standard keyboard.

At a microscopic level the brain is an astonishingly elastic structure. Every skill we acquire, every memory we store, is the result of new connections – and the brain makes new connections in seconds and new nerve pathways in minutes. In fact, as long as it is stimulated properly, it goes on making new connections right up until death.

The brain you have after learning a new language is different from the brain you had before. The brain you have after witnessing a jumbo jet crash in flames in a crowded shopping mall is different from the brain you had just seconds before. Life changes our brains all the time.

It changes them even as they are being formed in the foetus. The 10,000 or so interconnections that every neuron is capable of making begin in the womb, enabling every new-born baby to breathe, eat, excrete and recognise its mother at the very least.

It doesn't remain a mere mammary docking module for very long, however. The connections increase dramatically over the next few years as the child learns to walk and talk. There is another 'population explosion' of connections as the child enters adolescence and maturation.

Poets tell us that adolescence is springtime – leaf and blossom appear, and vines burgeon with the promise of fruit to come.

The reality is not so innocent and simple: beneath the surface there is din and clamour as the brain

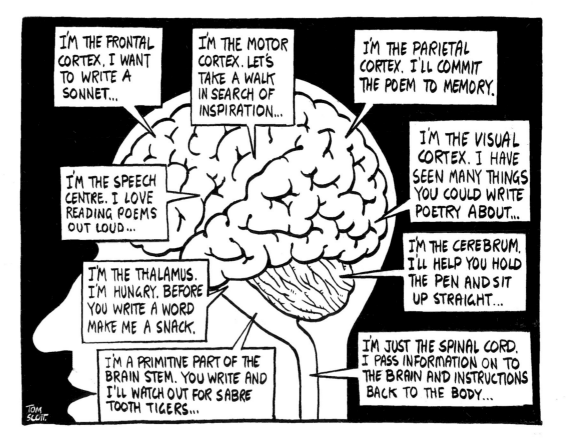

reinvents itself, then reinvents the body. No audible sounds emerge from this secret electro-chemical world as it transforms child into adolescent and adolescent into adult.

Imagine the largest stock exchange that ever existed at opening time during a bull market. 100 billion dealers are buying, selling and exchanging shares making deals, cancelling deals, off-loading old plant, investing in new plant, recording information, analysing information, discarding redundant information, permanently storing vital information, anticipating market trends, and making split-second decisions, like whose turn it is to make the coffee.

Brain activity is something like that – and it's all mute. The mental trading is done with nods, winks and subtle signs. Chemicals move in and out of nerve cells, and tiny electrical currents whizz up and down nerve pathways. All thinking, feeling and acting is a consequence of the 100 billion cells doing deals with each other.

Any foreign substance that interrupts the nods, winks and subtle signs retards or impairs this secondary evolution of the brain, robbing a child of its full potential. The consequences can be very devastating – the equivalent of a Wall Street crash.

A QUIET DAY IN THE SECONDARY EVOLUTION OF THE BRAIN...

VANDALISM IN THE REFINERY

WHAT DRUGS CAN DO TO THE BRAIN

Until recently, no one knew quite why chewing the leaves of a small shrub found growing high in the Andes gave the chewer a sudden rush of energy. Or why licking the skin of a certain species of tropical toad caused hallucinations. Or why igniting the leaves of some plants and then inhaling the smoke elevated your mood.

The short answer to all of the above is that there are thousands of chemicals in nature with properties similar to the brain's own mood-altering chemicals.

When these naturally occurring chemicals are ingested or inhaled, they enter the bloodstream and travel to the central nervous system, where they mimic, or inhibit, the actions of the brain's own mood-altering chemicals.

The greatest manufacturer and user of mood-altering chemicals on the planet is the human brain. Every second of your life, your brain is manufacturing its own drugs, distributing its own drugs, dealing its own drugs and consuming its own drugs. These are the neurotransmitters.

The brain's own drug factories are located at the end of axons. Although the amount of neurotransmitters needed at each synapse is minuscule, there are upwards of 100,000,000,000,000 synapses to service, so the brain's own drug tab with itself adds up.

Many central nervous system disorders are caused by imbalances in the functioning of neurotransmitters or a deficiency in the specific nutrients needed for their manufacture.

In extreme emotional states like schizophrenia, rage, terror or despair, the brain is literally overdosing on some of its own drugs. In other states, such as Parkinson's disease and suicidal depression, the brain is literally going

> A drug is a substance that when injected into a guinea pig produces a scientific paper.
>
> *L & M Cowan*
> ***The Wit of Medicine***

through withdrawal as it runs out of certain neurotransmitters. Fasting and malnutrition will limit the quantity of neurotransmitters that the brain can replenish. So will sleep deprivation.

Some neurotransmitters, such as the endorphins – feel-good chemicals – have become stars in their own right and have entered the popular consciousness. The most humble weekend jogger is now able to proudly defend his painful-looking shuffle on the grounds that endorphins are giving him a runner's high.

Long before endorphins were discovered, scientists postulated that if chewing opium leaves made people feel good, then the brain itself must have naturally occurring opiate receptors and naturally occurring opiates triggering them. Blood tests confirm that aerobic exercise, sex, laughter, listening to a favourite piece of music, or listening to a good preacher, a good therapist or a good coach are all capable of raising endorphin levels.

In one sense our brains are little more than vast refinery complexes filled with tanks, vats and reservoirs of transmitters. Our thoughts, feelings and acts are governed to some extent by which vats are filled to overflowing and which reservoirs are close to empty. Mood-altering drugs work by indiscriminately puncturing and draining the various vats and reservoirs.

When transmitter tanks are drained, supplies have to be built up again from dietary amino acids. People who consume huge quantities of noradrenalin by expending

We understand how folk medicine worked with plants. People were eating plants anyway. They noticed that some of them tasted good, some of them made them sick, and some of them made them want to lie around all day listening to the Doors through headphones. *James Gorman, The Man With No Endorphins*

physical energy, concentrating hard on intellectual tasks or by taking stimulants rarely declare 'Jeez, I could do with a huge dose of tyrosine and phenylalanine' (the dietary amino acids needed by the brain to manufacture noradrenalin). Instead, they reach for more stimulants, which only further depletes the tanks – slowly, in the case of a cup of coffee, a lot more quickly in the case of substance abuse.

A HEALTHY INDIVIDUAL CAN KEEP ALL OF HIS OR HER NEUROTRANSMITTER TANKS TOPPED UP BY:

♦ *maintaining a nutritious diet rich in vitamins. The 10 essential amino acids in children and eight essential amino acids in adults, and the lecithin and choline needed to make the neurotransmitter acetylcholine.*

♦ *avoiding chronic stress. Like the permanent pain of rheumatoid arthritis or chronic migraine, chronic stress depletes tank levels.*

♦ *getting a decent night's sleep. It is during sleep that the body manufactures and replenishes the transmitters, which is why sleep deprivation is the basis of brainwashing. The tank levels go down and defiance rapidly becomes compliance. Even broken sleep can profoundly alter moods, as the parents of newborn babies know only too well. After five nights of interrupted sleep, a parent who graduated with honours in the sensitivity section at pre-natal class can become a snarling selfish monster.*

Some clinicians say we shouldn't call anybody a marijuana or heroin addict or an alcoholic: we should really say that they are suffering from a neurotransmitter deficiency syndrome.

If an individual's vats containing the chemicals responsible for calm and moderation are nearly empty, and at the same time the vats containing the chemicals responsible for irritation and rage are full, the chances of their responding sensibly to a minor setback or mild confrontation are that much more remote. The response is more likely to be disproportionately aggressive.

Look around you. Our television screens, newspapers and radios are filled with stories of crimes that leave us wondering what drove this or that person to commit some

unspeakable act. Neuroscience is increasingly providing some of the clues.

A number of studies have found, for instance, that people with a history of violent behaviour have lower than usual serotonin levels in the brain. Serotonin is a neurotransmitter involved in nerve pathways responsible for self-esteem, appetite control and memory among other things.

The human male – the most needlessly aggressive animal on the planet, particularly between the ages of 15 and 25 as road toll statistics attest – has the highest blood levels of the hormone testosterone. And testosterone carried in the bloodstream to the brain is a mood-altering substance that raises libido as it lowers serotonin levels. Nature cruelly heightens libido in young men and makes them giddy with sexual longing at the very time it deprives them of the confidence to do anything about it.

Despite the vast array of neurotransmitters operating in the brain, and the vast array of substances that can mimic or contradict their function, there is a terrible sameness in the language of substance abusers. The same themes repeat themselves and we should take them at their word:

'I got plastered.'

'I got legless.'

'I got pissed as a newt.'

'I got shit-faced.'

'I got off my face.'

'I got high.'

'I got stoned.'

'I got zonked.'

'I got totally out of it.'

'I got blown away.'

'I got ripped.'

'I got smashed.'

'I got blasted.'

'I got wasted.'

THERE IS A CLEAR PATTERN HERE:

1. Users have difficulty expressing themselves.
2. Demolition is a recurring motif. This is no accident: unwittingly they are describing exactly what is happening to their own neurons.

Analogies do not constitute proof, but they can be useful. If for a moment you imagine the human brain as a shopping mall, alcohol and solvent abuse could be likened to young punks strolling casually through the arcade shattering every plate-glass window with a length of pipe.

Cocaine and heroin are urban guerrillas who toss Molotov cocktails into the entranceway. Loud explosions rock the building. Alarms squeal, sprinklers gush and there is general pandemonium.

Lysergic acid diethylamide (LSD) is a demented graffiti artist with delusions of genius who sprays preposterous images in fantastic colours across every surface. At first glance you can't tell door from window, or floor from ceiling.

Marijuana is a cat burglar. It enters the mall quietly, finds the shop responsible for memory, picks the lock, deactivates the alarm systems and slips inside. Once there, it unscrews the back of every piece of electronic equipment in the place and starts snipping leads and wires at random. It exits just as stealthily, leaving no trace. In the morning everything looks okay but nothing works properly.

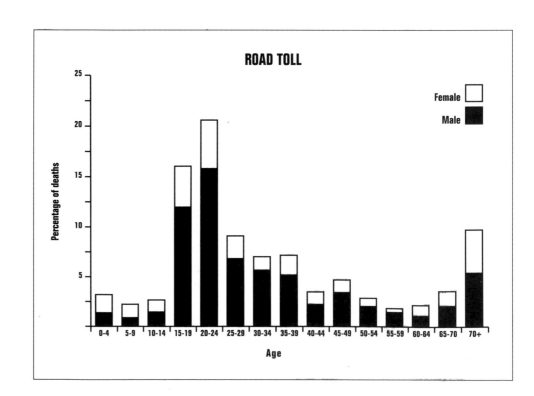

YOU MUST REMEMBER THIS

DRUGS AND MEMORY LOSS

All of what we know about the world that went before us, the world we live in now and our particular place in it – all of that, we have had to learn.

L earning is the process by which we acquire new knowledge. Memory is the process by which we retain that knowledge over time.

The actual mechanics of how and where memories are made and stored has been the subject of much scientific debate. The precise details are still being hotly contested but there is broad acceptance that when you learn something new, the information is somehow etched into your cerebral circuitry at incredible speed.

A unique pattern of neurons is quickly forged together – and if exposure to the event is repeated, and the event itself is significant, the constellation of synapses will be strengthened.

Memory is the steady, yet selective accumulation of the present. What is happening to you right now will become memory just a few seconds later. Learning and memory are central to our sense of individuality, and loss of memory leads to loss of contact with one's immediate self, one's life history and other human beings.

All incoming sensory information – from sight, sound, taste, touch, smell – goes to a critically important clearing-house in the brain called the hippocampus, which helps convert immediate experience into short-term memory and short-term memory into

Sticks and stones may break my bones, but names will never hurt me.

The sentiments of the 'Sticks and Stones' homily are noble but the reverse is true. Physical pain, while uncomfortable at the time, is usually quickly forgotten, whereas insults can burn themselves into our memories like branding irons. They can keep us awake at night years later, and in extreme cases we take them fresh and vivid to our graves.

I think, therefore I am.

René Descartes

permanent memory.

The hippocampus is particularly susceptible to damage from many mood-altering substances. A diminished hippocampus leads to diminished memory. Making sense of the immediate past becomes difficult. Making sense of the immediate future is problematic too.

In severe cases, people can be trapped permanently in the present, which in essence is what happens with Alzheimer's disease.

The one good thing about Alzheimer's is that you're always meeting new people.

Alzheimer's sufferer Ronald Reagan

In 'Strawberry Fields Forever' John Lennon sang that 'nothing is real'. If you are in a philosophical frame of mind and it's late at night and you've endured a pretty meaningless sort of day, this proposition has considerable appeal. If, however, you strike your thumb with a mallet at this juncture it becomes exceedingly difficult to sustain the notion that reality is just a figment of the imagination.

Reality is what we are experiencing now – measured against what we already know and what we expect the world to be.

People don't usually take drugs with the single intention of losing all contact with their immediate reality – unless of course they are desperately tired, in which case they can take sleeping pills.

People take drugs to modify and enhance their immediate relationship with reality. Like every other experience you've ever had, this altered perception of reality is duly recorded, if only temporarily, in the memory.

All that you experience, even altered perceptions of reality, has to be sorted and ordered by the hippocampus. Important experiences are set aside for permanent storage. Seeing a jumbo jet crashing into a shopping mall would come into this category. Other experiences are either placed in the 'matters pending' tray or shredded within hours. Remembering what side of the handbasin you placed your toothbrush this morning would come into the latter category. Remembering where you put the car keys the night before comes somewhere between matters pending and shred immediately.

The key to all learning, be it a poem you are trying to memorize or a new skill you would like to acquire, is repetition. When the 'matters pending' tray is filled to overflowing with the same

Images of faces, the plots of a thousand novels and movies, the way bacon tastes and coffee smells — how do we remember all these things? And where does our memory reside? We can hear a melody for only a few seconds and yet carry it with us for a lifetime. Experience somehow leaves its mark on the mind. But how can something as fleeting as song take on substance and become part of the brain, part of the body? How do we carry the past around in our heads?

George Johnson
In the Palaces of Memory

experiences, the brain takes the hint and stores the information long-term. A circuit left unused will eventually unravel, and attempted reactivation will retrieve a rough and faded memory at best.

By repeatedly taking mood-altering chemicals and repeatedly altering your perception of reality you start to store debased memories, and the process of losing contact with your immediate self is set in motion.

Accumulating debased drug memories is serious enough: even worse is that some mood-altering chemicals continue to debase memory and learning well after the particular high, fix, hit or what-have-you has worn off. If the mood-altering chemicals permanently damage the hippocampus, then memory and learning is permanently impaired.

THE BRAIN OF R.B.

R.B., a retired Southern California postal worker, in the aftermath of a coronary bypass operation suffered a sudden loss of blood to his brain. Though he survived with most of his faculties intact, he lost his ability to remember. He could recall events that had happened in the years before the operation, but he could not form new memories.

When R.B. died in 1983, his last half-decade an amnesiac blur, three scientists were allowed to dissect and study his brain...

R.B.'s amnesia had not been caused by massive or even moderate brain damage, they discovered, but by a tiny lesion in the hippocampus.

George Johnson
In the Palaces of Memory

WHAT IS MARIJUANA?

THE FACTS ABOUT CANNABIS *

Marijuana comes from the Cannabis sativa *plant, which can be easily grown in warm and temperate climates anywhere in the world. It grows wild on the roadside in Kathmandu, and can be cultivated hydroponically at the South Pole.*

In ancient times, its fibre was used to make clothing and rope, and for many centuries cannabis was used widely throughout Asia, the Middle East and North Africa as a medicine, as well as for its psychoactive properties.

The plant is tough, and particularly resistant to insects and disease. One way to get rid of it, though, is to turn it on itself: resin taken from the stem and injected into the root system will kill the whole plant.

Unique to *Cannabis sativa* are the resinous substances found in the stem, leaves and flower heads – the 62 cannabinoids. The most active,

Frequent marijuana use leads to more tissue destruction and long-term impairment of our highest intellectual functions than almost any other drug of abuse.

*Robert Gilkeson, former director
Brain Research Centre, California*

* See also the entry under MARIJUANA in the reference section, page 92, which covers the same ground as this chapter but in fuller and more scientific detail.

the most studied and the one that occurs in the highest concentration is the psychoactive agent Delta-9 tetrahydrocannabinol, commonly known as THC. This is the mood-altering chemical ingredient that induces mild euphoria, relaxation, time distortion and an intensification of ordinary sensory experiences.

Today's joint could be anywhere between five and 50 times more potent than its 1960s predecessor.

CANNABIS CAN ALSO PRODUCE THE FOLLOWING:

ACUTE SIDE EFFECTS

♦ Reddening of the whites of the eyes.

♦ Dry throat.

♦ Heightened appetite (the 'munchies').

♦ Anxiety, panic and paranoia, especially in naive users.

♦ Impairment of short-term memory, concentration span and psychomotor function, increasing the risk of an accident if you drive a vehicle or operate machinery when stoned.

♦ Possible psychotic symptoms such as hallucinations.

CHRONIC SIDE EFFECTS

♦ Probable respiratory diseases.

♦ Possible cannabis addiction.

♦ Memory damage and decline in other intellectual skills.

♦ Increased risk of cancer of aerodigestive tract.

♦ Increased risk of developing schizophrenia.

♦ Increased risk of leukaemia and birth defects in the children of women who used cannabis during their pregnancy.

♦ Marked decline in occupational performance in adults, and educational underachievement in children.

♦ Reduced output of reproductive hormones, leading to impaired ovulation, sperm production and libido.

♦ Lower white blood cell production and impaired immune system.

The concentration of THC varies between the three common forms of cannabis available on the market:

Marijuana is prepared from the dried flowering tops and leaves of the harvested plant. Potency depends on growing conditions and the genetic characteristics of the plant: THC concentration can range from 0.5 to 5 percent. (Sinsemilla – marijuana made just from flower heads – may have from 7 to 14 percent.)

Hashish, made from dried cannabis resin and compressed flowers, has a THC concentration ranging from 2 to 20 percent.

Hash oil, a dark, highly potent, viscous substance is obtained by extracting THC from hashish or marijuana with an organic solvent and concentrating the filtered extract. The THC concentration ranges from 15 to a staggering 50 percent.

Given that users may mix all three forms together, trying to compute the strength of an average dose is a thankless task. All that can be said with any certainty is that over the past 30 years the selective breeding of hybrid varieties of *Cannabis sativa* has increased THC concentrations in the leaves and flower heads to the point where today's joint could be anywhere between five and 50 times more potent than its 1960s predecessor.

When parents exclaim, 'Hey, I used to smoke the stuff all the time when I was at university, and look at me, I've got a law degree,' they are talking about a substantially different plant. Back in 1969, if you wanted to take in the same amount of THC as today's users regularly inhale, you'd have had to suck on a joint the length of an axe handle.

Marijuana is a widely used illicit drug in many Western countries. Surveys typically report that just over half of all males and about a third of all females have tried it. Usage is highest in young men aged between 15 and 24.

The most common way to absorb it is by smoking. Used orally, THC may take more than an hour to enter the bloodstream, but it is more potent and longer-acting. Upon inhalation, it enters the bloodstream in minutes, and may be active in the nervous system long after it ceases to be detectable in the blood.

THC moves easily into the membranes surrounding every cell in the body. In pregnant women, it slips across the placental barrier and into the foetal bloodstream. Likewise, in breastfeeding mothers THC crosses easily into breast milk.

In high concentrations, THC molecules clog cell membranes, making it difficult for nutrients to enter and for other substances to move out. This inevitably tends to lower cellular metabolic efficiency – i.e., the way the machine of the body runs. Less efficient cells in the testes produce less of the hormone testosterone, which in turn lowers sperm count and sex drive. Less efficient cells in the cerebral cortex make people less smart. Less efficient cells in the cerebellum make them less physically coordinated. Less efficient cells in the hippocampus mean a poorer memory.

THC's anti-nausea properties, useful in some clinical circumstances, can be fatal when combined with alcohol. Teenagers who smoke a joint or two and also drink heavily suppress their vomiting reflex and imbibe alcohol in quantities that would normally make them ill. Excessive blood alcohol results in uncontrolled anaesthesia, which can end in coma or death.

Growing old, feeble and infirm is part of life, and in the normal course of events it should take you a

He not busy
being born is
busy dying.

Bob Dylan

lifetime to get there. Sir William Paton, Professor of Pharmacology at Britain's Oxford University, quoted a British study that found brain atrophy in youthful heavy marijuana users equivalent to people aged 70 to 90.

To date, clear-cut, quantitative neuro-anatomical evidence of brain ageing in the hippocampus has been found in connection with chronic exposure to only one drug of abuse – and that is THC.

A growing number of scientific studies have confirmed the detrimental effect of THC – see the entry under MARIJUANA, page 92. It is important to deal here, however, with one particular argument commonly used in defence of marijuana.

MARIJUANA AS MEDICINE

In ancient times marijuana was used to treat a variety of illnesses, and today many marijuana users swear by its healing powers. Throughout the past two decades there has been strong and growing political pressure on American state and federal legislatures and on the DEA (Drug Enforcement Agency) to reschedule natural marijuana as a medicine.

Despite this clamour for change, the American Medical Association, the American Cancer Society, the American Academy of Ophthalmology, the National Multiple Sclerosis Society and the Food and Drug Administration all state that marijuana has not been found to be an effective and safe medicine, and petitions to reschedule marijuana have failed. The British Government remains opposed to the legalization of marijuana.

The process by which drugs are approved begins with studies of their chemistry, pharmacology and toxicology. A potential drug has to undergo rigorous clinical trials to test safety and efficacy – first in animals, then in human volunteers and later in patients.

The immediate difficulty with marijuana is that it is not a pure substance – every plant is different. Marijuana is an unstable, varying, complex mixture of more than 400 chemicals, many of which are unstudied either alone or in reaction to each other.

To avoid these complications a prescription drug called Marinol, made of synthetic THC, was approved by the Food and Drug Administration in 1985 as an anti-emetic agent (anti-nausea drug) for chemotherapy patients. In 1992 it was given further approval as an anti-anorexic agent for patients with AIDS wasting syndrome.

Because of serious side effects, however, prescription Marinol comes with an information sheet warning that: *'Marinol is highly abusable and can produce both physical and psychological dependence, hallucinations, depression, panic, paranoia. It causes decrements in cognitive performance and memory, decreased ability to control drives and impulses, and impaired co-ordination. Persons using the drug are instructed to be closely supervised by a responsible individual and not to engage in any activities requiring sound judgement. A full-blown psychosis may occur in patients receiving doses within the lower portion of the therapeutic range.'*

And that's just the synthetic variety. If all actual cannabis offered for sale in school playgrounds or all joints passed about at parties came with the same warning, doubtless there would be nowhere near as many takers.

THE STORY OF TWO USERS

'WE KNEW WE WERE SICK'

We started using drugs in the third form. At first it was just casually, for the usual reasons – curiosity, experimentation, rebellion. We believed that if we smoked drugs and drank in excess we weren't conforming.

To us that was what we were – rebels, non-conformists. We wanted to be different. Everything we could do to not conform, we did. At our school they pushed hard for conformity, e.g., everyone played rugby. The boarding masters sometimes forced us to do weights so we would play better rugby. As we were boarders we had constant pressure to conform 100 percent of the time.

It was very boring at the boarding school so we needed to do things a little on the 'naughty' side to keep our spirits raised. The thrill of almost getting caught, or getting caught and being caned, then telling our girlfriends how sore our arses were – these were our main sources of entertainment.

When we started smoking dope, drugs were cool, we were respected and we felt different. Probably this was our goal – to feel different. We would get our drugs from the gangs and we made contact with a powerful couple who were known in the supplying world.

After beginning drugs we went downhill quite quickly. We wagged school to get stoned and stole money from our parents and friends, or conned other students out of their money to get stoned and out of it. We felt we were doing everything at 110 percent.

We smoked every joint as though it would be our last – every toke would be as hard and long as we could make it. We used as much dope as we could get in the shortest period of time. We never saved any for after but we always managed to get enough money a few hours later, or met someone who we knew would stake us (our speciality). Our wanting to do schoolwork was

> We knew our parents were emotional wrecks... Thinking back, this part makes us feel sick.

gone and we couldn't remember yesterday's lessons anyway.

We worshipped people like Bob Marley, Robert Plant and Jimmy Page, whom we believed smoked more dooby faster and harder than anyone else. We thought that if you got high enough you would 'break through' and be enlightened, be given knowledge and special power. This is what we thought had happened to Led Zeppelin. We got so involved in the music that we started believing that we were the next Robert Plant and the second Jimmy Page. If only we could get high enough, we could be it – do it.

After a while we started having secret lives. We would have places that we could go and get stoned where no-one else could go, and we had a couple of user girlfriends we wouldn't let anyone meet. We started tripping LSD with them and taking a few pills. When this started happening we would try to learn each other's inner secret thoughts.

We became renowned for our lifestyle. If people our age and their parents hadn't met us, then they had almost certainly heard stories. In the dormitory there were three

of us – Jeremy, Bart and Ben. Ben, at this time anyway, never got into drugs or even cigarettes seriously. We thought we were the energy of the dormitory. We started school jargon – cool things to say, which other students made part of their vocabulary. We would giggle and laugh and talk at night till we dropped asleep. Generally we would have about two or three hours' sleep a night.

Things started to get really bad and we began to feel paranoid. We had different alibi systems, and our parents kept bugging us, along with the police. We left boarding school on a very bad note. Jeremy was sent to Palmerston North and Bart was sent to Masterton. We kept in contact by phone. We were fairly loyal to each other and we both enjoyed the limelight and the newborn freedom we had, being able to break free from the negative remarks and rules we faced from the school and our families.

We would meet other crazy people who told us we were amazing and really worth getting to know. Though separated, we supported each other, and our energy was

being poured into the drug lifestyle. When stoned we felt we could laugh anywhere, do anything, any time. Others thought we were pretty cool, with great stories to tell. Some of our friends started using because they thought we were fun. Some asked us to take them to one of the places in our stories to try drugs with us – the top of Mount Victoria, or the museum and other places. This hurts us a lot now when we think about it. We knew our memories were affected and it was embarrassing when we told lies and couldn't remember.

When we were at school we ran away, and when we left we would run away from home. We both had our own reasons – but we think the bottom line was that we knew we were sick and getting sicker of what was happening around us. When we were caught and taken back home we were angry at being caught but happy that something might happen. Neither of us could see a future.

By this time we were getting stoned every single day. The police referred us to a counsellor. We both went to see the counsellor, and were very interested, but we

**Carrington Briggs cared not two figs,
whether he lived or died.
But when he was dead he sat on his bed,
and he cried, and he cried, and he cried.**

Spike Milligan

still wanted to have fun and we were set in our ways. We knew our parents were emotional wrecks. Our relationships with our parents and families deteriorated completely. We almost never talked without fighting. Thinking back, this part makes us feel sick.

Gradually we had lost all our fun. Our spirits were low. Even talking to each other on the phone was hard. We felt troubled. We were always troubled with something, we couldn't concentrate on anything and we always felt tired. We had to pump ourselves up to have any energy at all. Any spirit we did have was false. We decided the scientific information the counsellor had given us was right, and we knew we had to try and give up using.

After we had given up for a while, we went back to the counsellor to see if he would help us stay on track. He seemed so pleased and positive when we met him, and we got a natural high about the feelings of hope he gave us.

After a period we started to notice things we hadn't seen for ages, feeling things we hadn't felt in years. We felt high on freedom from drugs and we agreed it was like being stoned – the new freedom.

After a further period we started experiencing withdrawals, depression about not being able to do anything with our lives. We did nothing for months, then finally through the counsellor we found employment.

Sometimes we met people we did drugs with, and when we told them we were clean of everything, they would smile and say, 'Yeah.'

We felt we had finally broken through and finished the drug journey, and were now the guru old men of drugs. We feel we are winning – we have jobs, we are saving, there are no more lies and no more false bullshit. We have formed normal relationships with our parents and friends. We have restarted our lives and are getting back some of the magic feelings that are a much better buzz.

– *Bart and Jeremy*

SO WHO'D BE A PARENT?

WHEN KIDS PUSH THE LIMITS

When parents learn that their children are taking drugs their initial reactions include guilt, anger, shame, shock and disbelief. Someone has to be responsible – preferably not them. Along with blaming each other they often take issue with the informer and blame the school, a former spouse, the football coach, law enforcement agencies, society at large or the government of the day for good measure.

At the centre of this emotional whirlwind, parents feel isolated and alone. This isolation often contrasts with their children's position. Children taking drugs as part of a group openly discuss the difficulties they are having with parents and swap strategies on how to deal with them.

A popular device is to transfer responsibility back onto the adults:

'My dad is hassling me about a harmless joint, and while he's ranting and raving he has a glass of alcohol in his hand.'

'My mum is always arguing and fighting – I just want peace, man, so I get out of it.'

'My parents never listen, it's one-way traffic man, so I just get wasted.'

'Parents can talk – what's wrong with us having a few tokes when adults have stuffed up the planet anyway?'

There is just enough truth in the above remarks to make parents feel uncomfortable. The best defence against this sort of pre-emptive strike is education. Parents can't afford to be diverted from the issue of the dangers of drug abuse by the shrewd smokescreens thrown up by their adolescent children.

Ideally, that education begins with parents providing a good example to their children. Minors do not have the right to misuse legal substances or use illegal substances, because their parents or caregiver pour themselves a good stiff gin at the end of the day.

All families have their rows – especially when adolescents are around – and today in single-parent homes or homes where both parents work, there never seems to be enough time for round-table family discussions.

But when children get involved with drugs, parents have to find the time.

Adolescence is a time of experimentation, and most youngsters will push the limits to see how far they can go. A little rebellion can be healthy – but they have to know that some things are unacceptable and will not be tolerated.

At a time when their own boundaries are so vague, adolescents feel secure if other boundaries just beyond them are well defined. There is a measure of security in sensible limits based on values they share with their parents.

In the next chapter we look at ways of identifying and combating drug use in adolescents. But prevention is better than cure, so we also look at how to create the kind of environment in which the growing child will not even be tempted to try drugs. Or, if tempted, knows to leave well alone.

WHAT CAN WE DO?

DON'T JUST SIT THERE, MAKE A LIST

One of the most painful things a parent can endure is seeing a once bright, loving child fall hopelessly short of her or his full potential, or worse, seeing them lying full stretch on a mortuary table.

Society as a whole and parents in particular go to great lengths to protect children. We build fences around swimming pools so that toddlers won't fall in. We teach children to swim so that they won't drown. We insist that they wear safety helmets when riding bikes. We teach children about stranger-danger, how to cross busy streets, how to combat bullying, how to look after themselves in lots of ways. We spend a fortune on education, health care, clothing, sport, music, arts and recreation, yet we spend hardly any money on, commit little time to and devote minimal effort to drug education.

Drug use and abuse is potentially the most destructive activity that children can become involved in. In many communities the majority of crimes, many of the road accidents, most of the workplace accidents and absenteeism, are drug-related.

And the age of experimentation with drugs is getting younger: eight-year-olds are now at risk in some communities. Drug distribution has become more sophisticated, drugs are now more readily available, they come in a wider variety and their potency has increased.

Here are some things that you as a parent can do to minimise the risks:

♦ Be constantly vigilant in regard to your child's attitude.

♦ Be aware of your child's social environment.

♦ Find the time to be around your child's activities.

♦ Find the time to be an active listener. Turn off the TV, the radio and the stereo. Put

> Every time you pick up the tab for obnoxious behaviour, you have just paid for the next round.

down the book or newspaper and pay your child some attention.

♦ Be assertive and accommodating in your guidance.

♦ Be aware of where your child is at night and be awake when they come home.

♦ Get children involved in the family decision-making process.

♦ Tell them your concerns where appropriate. You are their role model, and if at times you feel inadequate, then share this with them and they will respond to your honesty and humanity.

♦ Encourage your child to play some sport; make sure he or she eats three healthy meals a day and gets plenty of regular sleep.

♦ Make sure your child feels needed, wanted and respected.

♦ Learn the telltale signs of substance abuse (see Chapter 2).

♦ When it becomes obvious that your child is in trouble, when the signs of substance abuse are irrefutable and you want to push the panic button, it's time to sit down and take a deep breath.

♦ Do not over react. Discuss the situation dispassionately with the whole family. Keep a constructive dialogue going with the child who's abusing drugs while you buy time to seek expert advice.

♦ Educate yourself on the real dangers of substance abuse. You will be in direct competition with some self-declared authorities in the playground and wider community. At this stage children and adolescents think they know more about drugs than you do, and

they are probably right. On the other hand, teenagers' drug education is given to them by drug dealers whose primary motivation is profit, or by users who get their supplies subsidised by new recruits.

♦ Remember your ultimate goal is to get your child off drugs. Half-measures will avail you of nothing. The child has to be told that abuse of drugs in any form is an abuse of the whole family. The whole family will bear the consequences of the lying, the stealing and the heart-break. Accordingly the whole family has a right to make some input.

♦ Parental discipline needs to be rational and sensible. Love has to be tough. Every time you pick up the tab for obnoxious behaviour, you have just paid for the next round.

♦ Contact the parents of friends of your child who might also be on drugs. Combined parent power is stronger than children's peer pressure groups. No-one – not even their best friends – loves your child as much as you do. If there is no parent group at your child's school, then start one with the help of the Parent Teachers Association.

♦ Work with and support principals, teachers, police youth aid initiatives and drug education programmes. Prevention can work when everyone works together. Most towns have a citizens advice bureau that can direct you to the experienced agencies in your area. Look them up in your telephone book. If dissatisfied with the help

they offer, you may need to widen your search.

♦ If your child has broken the law, you will probably agonise over whether or not you should notify the police. Mind you, while you're wringing your hands, there is every chance the police will eventually be notifying you. In some communities, contacting the police would be a retrograde step. Where you have enlightened law enforcement agencies, police intervention can be enormously beneficial.

♦ Contact your doctor, and if he or she says marijuana is nothing to worry about, then it's time to start worrying about your doctor.

♦ Treat with caution the gospel of some social scientists who insist that a 'safe' drug is merely a dangerous drug that a child or adolescent has not been taught how to use correctly. There is no such thing as children's safe use of addictive and harmful substances, just as there is no safe way to play Russian roulette.

♦ Avoid the 'you need me' drug treatment agencies that push the line that the drug problem will never go away, therefore our children need to be taught how to use drugs properly. This is a popular philosophy in some quarters, because it is what all users want to hear. An addict told that he can stay on drugs forever as long as he learns how to manage his addiction is hardly likely to opt for the rigours of total abstinence.

Your responsibility as a parent is not as great as you might imagine. You need not supply the world with the next conqueror of disease or major motion picture star. If your child simply grows up to be someone who does not use the word 'collectible' as a noun, you can consider yourself an unqualified success.

Fran Lebowitz

Because there can be no cure under this approach, therapists from this school of thought run no risk of running out of clientele; indeed, they are more likely to develop long waiting lists made up of addicts who can hardly believe their luck.

STAYING DRUG-FREE

If and when you make a breakthrough with your child, and he or she accepts the importance of delaying all decisions on drugs until they are through maturation, there are a number of things you can do to help them clear the drugs from their system.

♦ Ensure they eat three nutritious meals a day. A dietitian can advise you here. Adolescents need a well-balanced diet rich in minerals and vitamins to provide the brain and body with the nutrients essential to normal development.

♦ Encourage them to exercise in a sport they enjoy, ensuring they get up a sweat that will speed up the elimination of toxins from the body. Exercise increases the aerobic capacity of the adolescent, pushing essential oxygen to all areas of the body, stimulating growth, aiding digestion and facilitating the natural desire for a good night's sleep.

♦ Regular sleep is essential. Sleep is when the body's batteries are being recharged – when the next day's neurochemicals are being manufactured.

♦ Get them to drink lots of fluids to help flush out the system. Short courses of vitamins, especially B and C, can be very beneficial.

♦ Get them to practice deep breathing in fresh air. This will help to improve oxygen levels in blood travelling to the brain.

♦ Give them love based on mutual respect. Tell them repeatedly that you love them and that it is only the bad drug-induced behaviour that you loathe.

CHAPTER II

KIDS, THIS IS FOR YOU

20 WAYS TO SAY NO TO DRUGS

Giving advice to teenagers can be likened to attempting to slow a speeding locomotive with a horseshoe magnet. You know it's an almost hopeless cause, and it won't do your stress levels any good, but sometimes miracles can occur. Actually, most of what follows in this chapter isn't advice at all – it's what most adolescents know instinctively anyway.

Kids, this is for you:

♦ Look after your brain – it's the only one you've got.

♦ Be aware of your parents' concerns.

♦ Be aware of their efforts to provide for your needs in not always easy circumstances.

♦ Be aware of your parents' interests and hobbies.

♦ Be accommodating of your parents' guidelines.

♦ Respect your parents' rules, boundaries and curfews.

♦ Be aware that one day you will probably be a struggling parent, baffled by teenagers of your own.

♦ Delay decisions about the use of legal and illegal substances until you have completed maturation.

♦ Remember that the most crucial stage of the secondary evolution of the brain is still being acted out right into your late teens and early 20s.

♦ Chemical vandalism of the maturation process drastically reduces the 10,000 potential connections that your 100 billion neurons are capable of making. The less connections you make, the less of the essential you there is. You have everything to lose and nothing to gain by becoming a diminished version of what you could have been.

> Remember that as a teenager you are in the last stage of your life when you will be happy to hear that the phone is for you.
>
> *Fran Lebowitz*

CHAPTER 11

20 WAYS TO SAY NO TO DRUGS AT A PARTY WITHOUT FEELING LIKE A DWEEB

1. Not for me, thanks, I'm a dweeb.

2. No thanks, I'm driving.

3. I'd rather not – I was kind of hoping to use my brain to make a living.

4. Hey, I get high on life. Seriously though, I'm snorting toilet bowl cleaner at the moment, and I'd rather not mix my poisons – if you know what I mean.

5. No way. Last time I touched that stuff I went home, tidied my room, mowed the lawns and washed the car. It was really scary, man.

6. I'm on pretty heavy medication for schizophrenia, so I should decline. Funny – half of me wants to say yes and the other half wants to say 'Hi there, earthlings, I come in peace…'

7. Drugs? What drugs? Where? Oh, I see, that stuff right there. Jeez, I think I might have had enough already.

8. Sorry, I never touch anything I haven't grown, mixed, distilled or stolen myself. It's a little hang-up of mine ever since I sucked on what I thought was a throat lozenge at a fourth-form party and woke up as a sex slave on a Russian trawler operating out of Vladivostok.

9. The last time I did this it turned out to be horse tranquilliser. I sprained my ankle on the way home and it took me hours to persuade a panel of vets that I shouldn't be put down.

10. Oh boy. I'm taking a risk here. My short-term memory is pretty shagged as it is… I'm sorry, what were you offering me again?

11. I don't smoke. If you want to make me hash cookies, or better still, pavlova, I'm a starter, but don't go to any trouble.

12. Have you got anything that won't make me projectile-vomit without warning?

13. I can't. I'm an undercover cop. I'll have one at home when I'm off-duty.

14. You wouldn't really want me sharing that. I've got these weeping boils on my gums that just won't heal.

15. I'll pass. I have enough trouble getting erections as it is.

16. No thanks, my IQ is dangerously low already.

17. Pills scare me. The lady next door took liver pills all her life and when she died they had to beat her liver to death with a pick handle.

18. My probation officer wouldn't approve. He says the next time I pull someone's head off when I'm stoned I won't get off with periodic detention.

19. Have you got anything stronger? I mean, really strong. I'm into ECT right now. Smelling your own hair burning is really something else, man.

20. Call me wild and crazy, but I'm strictly a hot-milk-and-cocoa guy.

In point of fact, if you don't want to take drugs you don't have to explain or justify your actions to anyone. A polite but firm refusal is your prerogative. Better still, simply passing a joint or tab on to the next person without saying a word is a pretty powerful statement in itself.

A SISTER'S STORY

A SIBLING SLAYS THE DRAGON

I knew things weren't right, but I didn't know exactly what was wrong. I didn't see my brother as much as I used to, and put it down to the fact he was just too busy.

Then one day a mutual friend sat me down and said, 'Have you noticed anything about your brother lately?' What had I noticed? Nothing specific. He was more unreliable than he used to be, not that he was very dependable to begin with. He used to get on really well with my husband, children, and our Mum, but now he didn't seem to have the time nor the interest.

I had no answer to the question I had been asked. I had noticed lots of things and nothing. 'He's using.' That's all the friend said. In those moments everything changed. He may as well have said, 'Your brother's going to die.' To me it meant the same thing.

My older sister died of an overdose when she was 20. I was 18 then. Now my younger brother was going down the same track. How the hell could he do it? He loved her, he knew what happened, he even had a photo of her in his bedroom.

It is a curious thing, but I suspect the pain my brother felt in himself that led him to use drugs could not have been as great as the pain he then inflicted on himself as the using went on. Inevitably he also caused great agony to those around him.

All I could think about was how to save him. I figured the first thing I had to do was get him to admit what he was doing. I vainly hoped that if this was open between us he might stop, or when things got really bad he could come to me and I could look after him. I became obsessed with this idea and decided to confront him. I felt I only had one shot because if I failed then to get this thing in the open, he could shut me off forever, refuse to see me, refuse to talk to me.

So I asked him the question. 'Are you using?' Of course not. 'Then show me your arms.' (I realised later it could have been wrists, ankles, all sorts of places.) He wouldn't. I threatened to tell Mum what I

> Layered over the person we knew and loved was the hard shell of lies and ruthlessness an addict needs to survive.

suspected if he didn't own up. I threatened to tell the whole extended family. I threatened to tell the people he worked with. We argued round in a circle with lots of 'how dare you say that/do that/think that,' on both sides. Not only did I threaten him though, he threatened me, physically. I had cornered him and he was fighting. It was when he nearly hit me that I started to cry, and it was then he hugged me. For a moment I saw the brother I knew and loved.

If I had known what it would be like, I would never have confronted him in that way. It was a tortuous, anguished one hour hell that only those people you love a whole lot can ever put you through. But I brought that on myself. I was doing what I thought I needed to do, and so was he. Finally he said, 'Yes, I'm using, but you didn't hear me say that.' He promised to talk to me about it later and drove off. I knew he wouldn't talk later. His partner had been toughened up by using for years and she would never let him talk to me about it. Never admit it, that was the cardinal rule.

After that came two years of hell. I'd see him occasionally, always totally absorbed with himself and what he was doing. Family gatherings became a misery as with pinned eyes he and his partner fizzed and then fell into stupor.

Eventually, money became in short supply. It was going up his arms at an extraordinary rate. He was also trying to get a business going and was constantly looking for investors. He would come to see me with his schemes involving fantastic potential returns and opportunities of a lifetime. They were so close to production, all I had to do was give him a few thousand dollars and the profits would pour in. The plea was the same over and over.

He had all the pieces of paper looking right, all the words right and he looked the part – a smart young businessman founding a manu-facturing empire. Some pretty hardened bankers believed him too, but then they were missing a key piece of information. Creditors put caveats on family-owned property he had borrowed against without our knowledge, the debts climbed and the assets began to disappear.

As his life became increasingly desperate, everything that wasn't mortgaged was sold and everything that was mortgaged had reached the limit. He had borrowed as far as he could. Payback time was closing in on him.

One evening my mother phoned to say he had called, desperate and wanting to see her. He needed help. She was very concerned, but she couldn't take any more scenes with him. A moment later he phoned me, sounding very level but said he needed to see me that night, was 10 o'clock too late? I thought this is it, it's crunch time, he's hit bottom. Now he will come to me for help to get clean.

When he arrived he bore no resemblance to the son who had pleaded with his mother. He was back with another fantastic deal. It brought home to me the desperate game of manipulation he was playing. What was going to get the most money out of us? 'I need money to feed your grandchildren', or 'have I got a deal for you'.

I cried that night thinking it was for him, but it was for me. He was never going to come to me for real help. He was not going to give me the chance to save him. And if he did die it was going to be alone, away from us who loved him most.

To cut off someone you love is an agonising thing but every time we supported him in the way he wanted we merely helped him perpetuate his addiction and the shared nightmare that went with it. Layered over the person we knew and loved was the hard shell of lies and ruthlessness an addict needs to survive. It was when we got glimpses of the real person we used to know hiding inside that it shattered us. The kind and generous person we used to know was killing himself and we couldn't save him. The addict we had come to know was a horrifying distortion with a clearly defined list of priorities.

Drugs, money, drugs, money.

Through the hell years I ran a pretty constant harassment. I kept it in his face and he hated me. I was hurting him. It made no difference to what happened. Sometimes I wanted him to die, the grief was already so great. I got counselling which helped. I cultivated a stomach ulcer and heart trouble which didn't help. Now I wish I had loved him more and harassed and hurt him less during that time.

As he slid to the bottom, every time the phone rang I was expecting either abuse or a call that told me he was dead.

I don't know what day it was that he decided to change his life. He announced he was going into treatment and took himself to detox then on to a treatment centre. At first we suspected it was to lull us into writing cheques. Any trust we had in him had been shattered long before.

He was away for five months. I did not see him during that time though Mum did. Then one day he was back, and I arrived home to find him sitting on the deck waiting for me. That was three years ago.

Initially it was a tenuous time

for all of us as wounds healed and we came to forgive and to know each other again. But soon I found it wasn't my old brother I got back, it was a new version, an improved version. The most caring and gifted soul emerged. He has a love and enthusiasm for people and life that is wonderful to be around. God, what a frightening and painful time, but it was the most miraculous experience, for all of us.

This is not his story, it is mine. His story is also about pain and anguish – it is just that we suffered from different sides. Now though, the joy is shared together.

– Anne

Footnote: *When I finished writing this I asked my brother to read it. It was a scary moment for both of us. Although we had come to understand each other we had never discussed specifics. We were both in tears at the end. I asked what had turned him round. He told me that one day he decided to listen to his heart.*

GETTING OFF DRUGS

ONLY YOU CAN CHOOSE

If you have been taking mind-altering substances for 12 months or more, there is every chance you will have been eating poorly during that period. Your diet will probably have been low in essential trace elements – in particular you will probably have an iron deficiency. Less iron means that your body makes fewer red blood cells, which in turn means that your blood carries less oxygen from the lungs to the rest of the body.

The burning of glucose gives cells their energy, but cells deprived of oxygen can't burn as much glucose as they would normally. Tired cells go about their housekeeping less efficiently. Nutrients are not pumped properly into cells – the groceries are not delivered - waste products are not pumped out – the rubbish is not collected.

To check this out and for other tests, you will need to see your doctor. Ideally, your parents or caregivers should organise this and go with you. If you are on your own, or if your parents or caregivers are not interested or use drugs themselves, you will have to make the appointment yourself.

Once there, insist on a full medical examination with a toxicology test including drug screening, a trace element test and the liver function test.

These simple, painless tests can save not only lives but many hours of handwringing and analysis working out why someone is suddenly behaving strangely.

People who sniff solvents risk poisoning from lead, polymers and toxins that can trigger aggression and depression. Anaemia alone will make some teenagers freak out.

You should also get the doctor to check your immune system and check you for sexually transmitted diseases.

Kicking drugs on your own is not easy. Kicking drugs with an army of therapists lending you support is not easy either. Basically, people get well when they, and they alone, elect to change their behaviour. But there are things you can do to help make that decision stick.

10 ACTIONS THAT WILL HELP YOU KICK DRUGS

1. Increase your fluid intake. Drink at least half a gallon of water or natural fruit juice a day. This helps to flush toxic substances out of your system. It will have you heading to the bathroom all hours of the day and night but wearing out the carpet is a lot better than chewing it.

2. You should take up some form of exercise that has you producing one good sweat a day. Regular exercise increases oxygenation of the blood, and sweating helps to flush toxins out of the body. Regular exercise will also help you to sleep better at night.

3. Learn some relaxation and deep-breathing exercises. Do them every morning and at night.

4. If you experience withdrawal symptoms, if you get a little sweaty and panicky, get into a warm shower and slowly lower the temperature. In most instances the anxiety will fade.

5. If you find withdrawal too much, then contact the younger members of support groups, such as Narcotics Anonymous and Alcoholics Anonymous. At no cost and with absolute confidentiality they will provide the peer support and friendship desperately needed by those who are badly addicted.

6. Take a short course of vitamin B6 and B12. Alternate a capsule each day for six to eight weeks, then follow that with a four-week course of 500mg vitamin C. Drug abuse suppresses the immune system and this will give your body a gentle boost.

7. Eat sensibly. A nutritious diet is cheap and is essential to the brain's and the body's recovery. After exposure to toxins, a short session with someone who knows something about diet would be invaluable.

8. Go to bed at a sensible hour and get a good night's sleep in a well-ventilated room. Avoid coffee and alcohol for several hours before going to bed. It is during sleep that your brain manufactures all the chemicals it will need the next day.

Despite the fact that the rest of your body – apart from the heart and the lungs – is resting, during sleep your brain sometimes requires as much oxygen as if you were playing tennis. Don't take sleeping pills – parts of your brain have to be wide awake if the rest of your brain is to sleep properly.

9. Treat yourself to safe hobbies and interests that will develop your motivational skills and enhance your enjoyment of life – be it in music, art, sport or whatever else takes your fancy.

10. When you make it, don't be afraid to pass on your hard-won knowledge and experience to any friend who needs to undertake the same journey. There is bound to be resistance at first, but if it works out you will have made a true friend for life, and you will be that much stronger yourself.

A COUNSELLOR'S STORY

THE THREE-MONTH CHALLENGE

The first thing I noticed about Jacob was his size. He was the tallest of the surly boys waiting for me in the headmaster's office the afternoon I was called in to help. He came from a typical New Zealand family, academically he was average, but he possessed truly remarkable ability in one particular sport that he loved.

He had represented his school in this sport and taken provincial titles as he progressed through the age groups. His rapid improvement ended at the age of 16 when he started using drugs.

He was suspended from a large high school along with six other students for marijuana and other drug use. Their teachers had observed dramatic changes in behaviour and attitude. After police investigations I was called into the school to assist. Two boys were ultimately expelled for possessing and distributing drugs. One is now dead as a result of a drug overdose; he was only 18.

All of the boys displayed diminished interest in schoolwork, arrogant and obnoxious attitudes toward parents and teachers and short-term memory loss. Jacob was ordered to counselling. He presented himself to me with a 'Who gives a shit?' attitude. Indeed, when I spelt out the seriousness of the situation to him, those were his very words. His provincial sports coach had also thrown him out of the team. This devastated Jacob, as it was the one thing he still seemed to care about.

Initial blood tests confirmed the use of marijuana and an hallucinogenic substance. When confronted, Jacob opened up and told me the whole story of the group's secret experimentations with drugs – the direct result of one of them purchasing a book from a Head Shop (a shop specialising in literature advocating drug use).

Jacob was permitted to return to the school

> The disciplines and rigours of top-level sport quickly sort out the dedicated from the medicated.

under strict conditions, which included counselling. It was a difficult and lonely time for him. He was missing his sport but his coach held his ground, insisting he would need to be clean for an extended period of time if he wanted reinstatement in the squad.

I struck up a strong bond with him. We agreed on a contract. I would help him with all his problems and in return, if after three months he remained drug-free, I would approach his coach about giving him another chance. He also had to show more respect for his parents and teachers, to submit voluntarily to random urinalysis tests and, whenever I said 'Jump!', he had to reply 'How high?'

Three months later, having kept his end of the bargain, Jacob was back in the provincial squad performing better than ever and setting his sights on a national title. The disciplines and rigours of top-level sport quickly sort out the dedicated from the medicated, and Jacob was starting to excel.

His training and travel costs began to mount. Coming from a decent family of modest means it became clear that cash would have to be found if he was going to fully realise his exceptional potential. I approached two businessmen for help. Impressed by the strength of character Jacob had shown in overcoming his drug problem, they generously provided the necessary sponsorship.

In 1994 all three of us were present and immensely proud when Jacob won two national titles. He has since represented New Zealand overseas and is now an Olympic medal prospect.

There are many heartbreaks and disappointments in counselling. Jacob was one of the success stories. To meet him when he was at a crossroads and to witness his recovery and the triumphant way he took control of his life again has been a truly gratifying experience.

– *Joseph*

We agreed that if after three months he remained drug free I would approach his coach about giving him another chance.

CHAPTER 15

CONCLUSION

This book has only one purpose: to equip children and adolescents, their parents, guardians, teachers, community agencies and society at large with some simple facts about some very complicated substances.

What adults choose to sniff, snort, smoke, ingest or inject into their bodies is not our immediate concern. It has to be assumed that adults have some choice over their own behaviour. In theory anyway, they should be capable of understanding the legal, physiological, mental and emotional risks they are taking when they abuse drugs.

Children and adolescents need to know that you can't buy euphoria – at best you can lease it temporarily, but the premiums are high. Life has to be faced head-on, on life's terms. If you use a week's supply of the body's own feel-good chemicals in a single afternoon, you go into pharmaceutical debt to yourself. There is no denying emotional pain or hurt, but the sorrow you mask today is the sorrow you experience with interest tomorrow.

Life is hard, but as a blues singer once said, if it weren't for the rocks in its bed, the stream would have no music.

I do not wish you joy without a sorrow,
Nor endless days without the healing dark,
Nor brilliant sun without the restful shadow,
Nor tides that never turn against your barque.

I wish you faith and strength and wisdom and love,
Goods gold enough to help life's needy ones.
I wish you songs but also blessed silence
and God's sweet peace when every day is done.

A poem carved on the wall of an 18th-century Baltimore church.

I know that most men can seldom accept even the most obvious truth if it would oblige them to admit the falsity of conclusions which they proudly taught to others, and which they have woven, thread by thread, into the fabric of their lives.

Leo Tolstoy

THE DANGER LIST

FROM ALCOHOL TO STEROIDS:
A READY-REFERENCE GUIDE
TO ALL THE MAJOR DRUGS

Alcohol

First the man takes the drink, then the drink takes a drink, then the drink takes the man.
Japanese proverb

Most people who drink alcohol find it a useful social facilitator, a normal part of occasions happy and sad, and they have no problems with it. For those addicted to its use, however, alcohol is the occasion.

SOURCE:
The product of the fermentation of complex carbohydrates and sugars in fruits, vegetables and grains.

HISTORY:
The first instance of alcohol abuse is recorded in the book of Genesis. (After the Great Flood, Noah got drunk and disgraced himself.) Alcoholic beverages of varying strength have been consumed all over the world for thousands of years, except in Islamic countries, where religion forbids their consumption.

NEUROTRANSMITTERS DEPLETED:
Gamma amino butyric acid (GABA).

BRAIN SITES AFFECTED:
Cerebral cortex, cerebellum and brain stem – particularly the breathing centre.

INITIAL MOOD ALTERATION:
Mild euphoria, relaxation and sedation.

ACUTE SIDE EFFECTS:
Intoxication, diminished hearing, diminished sense of responsibility, hangover.

CHRONIC SIDE EFFECTS:
Addiction, cirrhosis of the liver, memory impairment, reasoning impairment, Korsakoff's syndrome, foetal alcohol syndrome.

International statistics indicate that eight percent of those who drink alcohol will develop problems with it, and that each one of those victims will affect at least six other people.

When one is intoxicated with alcohol, it is immediately obvious to all those around you, even if you insist loudly that you are as sober as a judge. This denial is harder to maintain in the morning, when you are suffering from a pounding headache, bloodshot eyes, sweats, nausea, tremors, memory loss and dry heaves, and there is something that looks suspiciously like last night's supper glued to your jacket lapels. Unlike drugs such as marijuana and LSD, alcohol has the virtue of giving its user plenty of signals of the damage being done.

Numerous studies report that low – repeat, low – doses of alcohol increase blood flow, accelerate heart rate, step up the transmission of nerve impulses, and excite simple spinal and brain-stem reflexes. Performance of highly complex problem-solving tasks is improved, memory and concentration are sharpened, and creative thinking is enhanced.

Initially alcohol can make the world seem a better place. After a while, however, alcohol's sedative effects take over from the stimulation, the pleasurable effects are cancelled out, and the average drinker stops drinking. People who don't stop at that point have the capacity to make the world a far worse place.

The active ingredient is ethyl alcohol (ethanol), a clear colourless inflammable substance that can be made synthetically or produced naturally by fermentation of fruits, vegetables or grains.

An adult liver can metabolise up to 30 ml of alcohol an hour. (A can of beer, a glass of wine or a regular nip of spirits could contain from 15 ml to 30 ml of alcohol.) Drinking at a greater rate than this accumulates ethanol in the bloodstream.

Children and adolescents absorb alcohol faster than adults, and their livers metabolise it less efficiently. By their own admission many teenagers do not drink socially – they drink to get high, drunk, rat-faced, wasted etc.

Alcohol has a low molecular weight. It is highly water-soluble but less fat-soluble. Once consumed, alcohol is distributed throughout body water. Having less muscle and more fatty tissue than males, females have less body water for alcohol to move into, so it remains in the bloodstream in higher concentrations than for a male of the same weight. A British Medical Association study showed that one jug of beer will raise a male's blood alcohol level to 60 mg/100 ml but the female's to 135 mg/100 ml.

When taken orally it is rapidly absorbed into the bloodstream from the stomach and small intestine and travels directly to the liver, where much of it is broken down into acetaldehyde.

Alcohol is a very necessary article. It enables Parliament to do things at 11 at night that no sane person would do at 11 in the morning.

GEORGE BERNARD SHAW

If you had six drinks in an hour, one drink would be converted into acetaldehyde in the liver while the other five would slosh around in the bloodstream as ethanol.

Acetaldehyde is a poison. It acts as a cellular irritant and, in high concentrations, causes damage, spilling into the bloodstream and travelling to the brain, where it interferes with brain amines acting as neuro-transmitters. The various symptoms of acetaldehyde poisoning are known collectively as a hangover.

Persistent acetaldehyde poisoning causes liver cells to perform poorly: some die and are replaced with fat and fibre. This is cirrhosis of the liver.

The latest studies show that, over time, ethanol reduces the metabolic activity of the brain. It directly depresses the neurons of the respiratory centre in the brain stem, reducing oxygen uptake and making breathing less efficient.

When blood oxygen levels are progressively lowered, the first stage is euphoria. Then come sedation, drowsiness, sleep, anaesthesia, coma and death. Fortunately for the drinker it is very difficult to drink while you are sleeping, and only the supremely dedicated make it to the coma stage.

In 1953, the Welsh poet Dylan Thomas, returning to his New York hotel room after a drinking binge, proudly informed his girlfriend that he had just downed 18 whiskies in a row. He then fell unconscious, lapsed into a coma and died. (Alcohol may not have been the only culprit: the day before, Thomas's doctor had given him two morphine injections for a medical condition.)

Because it diminishes people's sense of responsibility, makes them more reckless, and can heighten rage and despair, intoxication is potentially life-threatening – especially when coupled with testosterone, the hormone of male aggression. Alcohol can be deadly if the intoxicated one is behind the wheel of a motor vehicle, is in possession of a loaded weapon, or wants to go white-water rafting at night. But deaths from actual alcohol overdose are rare.

They are more common when alcohol is combined with other drugs, particularly marijuana. One of the side effects of marijuana use is suppression of the vomiting centre in the brain stem.

An inactivated vomiting centre permits a drinker to consume alcohol in volumes that would normally have them spewing their guts out. The extra alcohol remains in the system at toxic levels, plunging the drinker into a coma and possibly death.

All of us, regardless of race, colour, creed or gender, have a stern, humourless voice somewhere in the back of our skulls telling us to sit up straight, to face the front and to mind our own business. It warns against staring down the front of girls' dresses or dancing suggestively with boys. It reminds us that we have work or school in the morning and that we should go to bed early.

The beauty of alcohol is that it shuts that voice up halfway through the first glass. The curse of alcohol is that after the fifth glass the blessed silence is sometimes broken by another voice insisting that if we put our foot down we can beat the train to the level crossing.

Some extreme alcoholics would rather drink than eat, and over time they suffer from a vitamin B (thiamine) deficiency. Thiamine is crucial in the metabolism of glucose – the brain's main fuel – and prolonged vitamin B deficiency causes brain damage known as Korsakoff's syndrome. Victims suffer from apathy, confusion and profound memory impairment.

In the womb the still-developing foetal liver is short on enzymes, rendering the unborn child particularly susceptible to toxins. The placenta serves as the unborn baby's stomach and lungs. It has a vast surface area permitting molecules in the mother's blood easy access to the foetal bloodstream. Ethanol and acetaldehyde, which cross unimpeded, can't be broken down, are not excreted by the undeveloped kidneys, and are thus free to wreak havoc and destruction at will – a condition known as foetal alcohol syndrome. Ethanol moves freely through breast milk to the feeding baby.

DRUNK AT A PARTY: 'Excuse me, do lemons have feathers?'

HOSTESS: 'No.'

DRUNK: 'I'm dreadfully sorry, I seem to have just squeezed your canary into my gin.'

Old Joke

ALCOHOL STREET SLANG NAMES.

BOOZE, JUICE, BREW, TURPS,

PISS, PLONK, SAUCE,

LUNATIC SOUP ETC.

Amphetamines

Speed Kills
Road Code

Amphetamines act on the brain and body in much the same way as the more toxic naturally occurring drug cocaine. As the latter was subjected to increasing restriction and eventual prohibition, its role as a stimulant was taken over by amphetamines.

SOURCE:
Amphetamines are synthetic compounds with similar stimulant properties to cocaine – in the body, they mimic adrenalin, noradrenalin and dopamine – but without any anaesthetic action.

HISTORY:
They were first synthesised by Los Angeles chemist Gordon Alles in the 1930s and marketed under the trade name Benzedrine. Amphetamine was the active ingredient in inhalers used in asthma treatment.

NEUROTRANSMITTERS DEPLETED:
Adrenalin, noradrenalin, dopamine.

INITIAL MOOD ALTERATION:
Amphetamines are powerful stimulants. They elevate mood, prevent sleep, suppress appetite and stave off fatigue.

ACUTE SIDE EFFECTS:
High blood pressure, strokes and (after large doses or an injection) overwhelming euphoria followed by devastating depression, exhaustion and confusion.

CHRONIC SIDE EFFECTS:
Addiction, fatigue, paranoia, psychosis.

During the Second World War the armed forces of many countries provided their soldiers and pilots with amphetamines – 'pep pills' – to combat fatigue, elevate mood and increase endurance. In Japan at the same time, amphetamines were widely distributed to civilians working in factories, and at the war's end Japanese drug companies unloaded their massive stockpiles onto the demoralised populace as the ideal way to 'replenish the spirit'. By the late 1940s, five percent of Japanese adults were dependent on amphetamines.

Elsewhere, particularly in America, 'pep pills' started appearing on the black market. Soon they were being used by students to help them study, truck drivers to stay awake on long hauls, and athletes to sharpen their performance.

In the 1950s American soldiers in Korea and Japan began mixing amphetamines with heroin to make 'speedballs' that were taken intravenously.

In the 1960s, amphetamines were prescribed by doctors for the treatment of depression, narcolepsy and obesity. Widespread abuse of 'diet pills' by housewives led to the re-examination of amphetamine use. The more it was studied, the more its dangerous similarity to cocaine use became apparent. Apart from the treatment of narcolepsy – a rare condition whereby sufferers spontaneously fall asleep – over the past 10 years there has been a marked decrease in the prescription of amphetamines by the medical profession; and sports bodies worldwide have banned their use by athletes.

But street demand and black-market distribution is still booming.

While amphetamine use elevates mood and increases alertness, it also reduces the body's natural stores of adrenalin, leading to fatigue, depression and paranoia, and increasing the risk of brain, heart and lung blood vessel rupture.

Little is known about amphetamine use and pregnancy. There is some evidence of a withdrawal syndrome occurring in babies born to women using amphetamines extensively.

Ritalin (methylphenidate) is a central nervous system stimulant. While chemically different to amphetamines, it has similar pharmacological properties. Developed as an anti-depressant and an appetite suppressant, Ritalin is now in vogue for the treatment of Attention Deficit Disorder (ADD). The authors are familiar with doctors working long punishing hours who have used Ritalin's stimulant properties to help them stay awake – an unsafe practice that has resulted in severe addiction and the need eventually to seek treatment. Parents treating their ADD children with Ritalin should be aware that in the family medicine cabinet there lurks a drug with a considerable potential for abuse.

AMPHETAMINES STREET SLANG NAMES.

'A', AMPH, BEANS, BENNIES, BILLY, MOLLIES, TICKLERS, BROWNIES, CARTWHEELS, CRANK, CRYSTAL, DEXIES, DIET PILLS, DOLLS, FOOTBALL, HEARTS, LID POPPERS, LIGHTNING, PEP PILLS, RIPPERS, SPEED, SULPHATE, UPPERS, UPPIES, UPS, WHIZZ AND A HOST OF OTHERS.

Barbiturates

She keeps running to the shelter of her mother's little helper.
Rolling Stones

Many psychiatrists define anxiety as a fear response in the absence of appropriate stimuli. Anxiety states can vary from the mild and disquieting to the severe and disabling. Barbiturates and benzodiazepines were developed to help treat anxiety.

SOURCE:
Synthetic – i.e., made in the laboratory.

HISTORY:
Barbiturates first came into use in the early years of the twentieth century. Benzodiazepines were first synthesised in the late 1950s and Valium – the most famous barbiturate – entered the market in 1963.

NEUROTRANSMITTERS DEPLETED:
GABA.

BRAIN SITE AFFECTED:
Gaba receptors in cortex and brain stem.

INITIAL MOOD ALTERATION:
Relief of anxiety and panic, sedation, sleepiness.

ACUTE SIDE EFFECTS:
Death from massive overdose, especially when combined with alcohol.

CHRONIC SIDE EFFECTS:
Crippling emotional and physical dependence, severe addiction.

In 1864 the Belgian chemist Adolph van Baeyer synthesised a powerful sleep-inducing drug from malonylurea and named it barbituric acid in honour of a friend called Barbara, who presumably was not the most animated person he had ever met.

In 1884 the first barbiturate for medical use – barbitone – was manufactured in Germany; in 1903 it was released for general use under the trade name Veronal.

Initially, barbiturates were used to induce sleep, replacing alcohol, bromides and opiates such as laudanum. Since then, thousands of barbituric acid derivatives have been synthesised. Most are highly and dangerously addictive. Until very recently, 'barbs' were the most used and abused of all the prescription drugs. These drugs, sometimes called sedative hypnotics, act as depressants in the brain, producing a calming, sleep-inducing effect.

They slow down the activity of the nerve pathways that control the emotions, breathing, heart action and some other functions. They work by mimicking or exaggerating the actions of the brain's own calming mechanism – the gaba (gamma amino butyric acid) neurotransmitters.

Barbiturates are broken down in the liver and eliminated by the kidneys at varying speeds according to their type. The slow-acting ones – mainly phenobarbitone and barbitone – reach the brain through the bloodstream in one to two hours. Their effects last six to 24 hours, with a half-life of 48 hours for phenobarbitone and 24 for barbitone.

The intermediate and fast-acting barbiturates – mainly secobarbitone and pentobarbitone – take effect in 20 to 45 minutes. The quick ones are the commonly known sleeping pills whose effects last only five or six hours, with little or no after-effects when not abused.

Barb abusers favoured this group because the effects are similar to alcohol – in speed of impact, intoxication produced and subsequent addiction. This group has been identified with many suicides. The ultra-fast-acting barbiturates – mainly thiopentone (sodium pentothal) produce unconsciousness in a

BARBITURATES/ANXIOLYTICS HYPNOTICS STREET SLANG NAMES

BARBS, BEANS, BENNIES, BLACK BEAUTIES, BLOCKBUSTERS, BLUE ANGELS, BRAIN TICKLERS, DOWNERS, GOOFBALLS, GREEN DRAGONS, MOGGIES, MOTHER'S LITTLE HELPERS, NEMBIES, NIMBIES, PHENNIES, PINK LADIES, PURPLE HEARTS, SLEEPERS, YELLOW JACKETS AND MANY OTHER NAMES.

matter of seconds, which explains why their main use is for anaesthesia in hospitals. Sodium pentothal is also used as a truth serum by American police and for veterinary use when putting a cat or dog down.

The effects of barbiturate abuse during pregnancy are similar to those of alcohol. The drug is carried in the bloodstream, through the placenta, to the foetus. After the birth the baby will suffer from the usual symptoms of barbiturate withdrawal and impaired development due to brain damage in the womb.

Psychological dependence on barbiturates can develop very quickly. Physical dependence takes longer but is far more dangerous. It occurs when the body has grown so used to the presence of the drug that it reacts violently if the drug is suddenly withdrawn. Physical dependence to barbiturates and other sedative hypnotic drugs is one of the most deadly of all drug dependencies.

The withdrawal symptoms are worse than those of morphine or heroin. Death occurs in about five percent of those attempting withdrawal without supervised treatment, and some withdrawal effects can last for months – yet despite the rigours and risks

of barbiturate withdrawal, there is no established barbiturate maintenance programme.

Barb users often use other drugs as well, such as amphetamines – the 'upper/downer' syndrome. Alcohol and barb use together can be fatal, as both drugs enhance each other's effects.

The prescription of barbiturates by the medical profession has declined over the last few years, but during the same period there has been a significant increase in the use of other anxiolytic hypnotics, particularly the benzodiazepines (the minor tranquillisers). These include Librium, Valium, Mogodon, Rohypnol, Serepax, Ativan, Notec and many others. All are potentially abusable and should only be used under strict medical supervision.

Two original claims made about the benzodiazepines by their manufacturers have since been discarded. First, it was claimed that, unlike barbs, they induced calm without sleepiness. It is now recognised that the benzodiazepines do induce sleep and that this property is dose-related.

Secondly, the new drugs were claimed to be non-addictive and would not induce the type of compulsive dependence syndrome associated with barbs. This claim eventually proved invalid, as numerous cases of compulsive dependence accompanied by a significant withdrawal syndrome are documented. Despite the inability of the benzodiazepines to live up to some of the early claims, they have virtually replaced the barbiturate in the treatment field for numerous conditions because they are less toxic and have far wider safety margins between the usual therapeutic doses and the amounts needed for fatal doses.

The benzodiazepines are found in most family medical cabinets. There is a growing trend of children taking leftovers to school for experimentation. Parents need to be mindful of the contents of medicine cabinets in their homes. Elderly women are the largest group receiving prescriptions for these drugs.

Rohypnol (flunitrazepam) is a hypno-sedative with the street name 'Roly' or 'Rollies'. It is also known as the 'date-rape drug'. Its use is increasingly widespread at teenage rave-ups. Sometimes it is proffered as ecstasy or acid. When mixed with alcohol, which is easily done at parties, its stuporific effects are dramatically enhanced – a fact not lost on unsavoury predatory males, who deliberately encourage this practice, as when young women become legless, getting them knickerless is not such a hard next step.

Being semi-comatose at a party is hardly the ideal state for a teenage girl to make an informed decision about whether or not to have sex. Girls who unknowingly accept party drinks spiked with powdered Rohypnol risk the possibility of rape, exposure to sexually transmitted diseases, and unwanted pregnancy.

As a powerful central nervous system depressant, Rohypnol is potentially a very dangerous drug if abused, especially when combined with other depressants like alcohol. Rather than just becoming semi-comatose, a number of young people have become completely unconscious, lapsed into a coma, and died from respiratory failure.

Caffeine

> There's no point giving a drunk coffee: you'll just end up with a wide-awake drunk on your hands.
>
> *Old adage*

The most popular drug in the world, caffeine is mainly consumed in tea and coffee but is also present in cola drinks, cocoa, certain headache pills, diet pills and patent stimulants.

DELICIOUS!

SOURCE:
Caffeine is a naturally occurring alkaloid found in the leaves, berries or seeds of six plant types: the coffee bush originating in Arabia and Turkey, the tea bush originating in China, the cola nut tree in West Africa, the cacao shrub originating in Central and South America, the cassina berry tree in North America, and the ilex plant in Brazil.

HISTORY:
The world's most widely used mood-altering drug. Preparations derived from the leaves of tea plants and coffee beans were introduced to Europeans during the exploration of the New World 500 years ago. Caffeine was first isolated from coffee beans in 1820, and then from tea leaves in 1827.

NEUROTRANSMITTERS DEPLETED:
Adrenalin, noradrenalin, dopamine.

INITIAL MOOD ALTERATION:
As caffeine is a stimulant, it elevates mood and alertness.

ACUTE SIDE EFFECTS:
Irritability, anxiety, panic, accelerated pulse, elevated blood pressure, diuresis, acid stomach.

CHRONIC SIDE EFFECTS:
Insomnia, persistent anxiety, breathlessness, gastric disorders, headaches, addiction.

Rapidly absorbed into the body, it reaches all body tissues in five minutes, peaks in the blood at 30 minutes, and has a half-life in the body of about three and a half hours. It is rapidly metabolised in the liver before being excreted via the kidneys. There is no day-to-day accumulation of the drug in the body.

Caffeine is a potent stimulant of the brain and heart muscle. Blood vessels in the brain are constricted, but the ones in the heart are dilated. Heart rate and blood pressure increase. Caffeine also acts as a diuretic, increasing urination, and stimulates the secretion of gastric acid in the stomach – the cause of 'heartburn'.

Its ability to constrict blood vessels in the brain has led to it being used as an ingredient in some prescription analgesics (mild painkillers) aimed at treating headaches caused by the dilation of blood vessels.

In neuroscience terms, caffeine works by helping to drain the tanks containing the brain's own naturally occurring stimulants – dopamine, adrenalin and noradrenalin. As well as being a stimulant, it causes mild anxiety by interfering with other nerve pathways served by the neurotransmitter GABA (gamma aminobutyric acid), which is the brain's naturally occurring sedative. By binding with and blocking GABA receptors, caffeine denies further transmission of soothing messages.

In moderate doses, caffeine postpones fatigue and increases alertness and talkativeness. Regular use of 350 mg a day leads to physical dependence. Interruption of use can lead to withdrawal symptoms, the most prominent of which is severe headache.

Regular use of more than 600 mg a day (approximately eight cups of percolated coffee) may cause chronic insomnia, breathlessness, persistent anxiety and depression, mild delirium and stomach upset. It may also cause heart disease. A John Hopkins University study found a modest association between heavy coffee drinking and rupture of the cardiac blood vessels in young women.

Studies have also shown that the heavy use of caffeine in amounts equivalent to eight or more cups of coffee a day is responsible for an increased incidence of spontaneous abortions and stillbirths.

Death from overdose is extremely rare, but 3.2 g administered intravenously would make short work of a sumo wrestler.

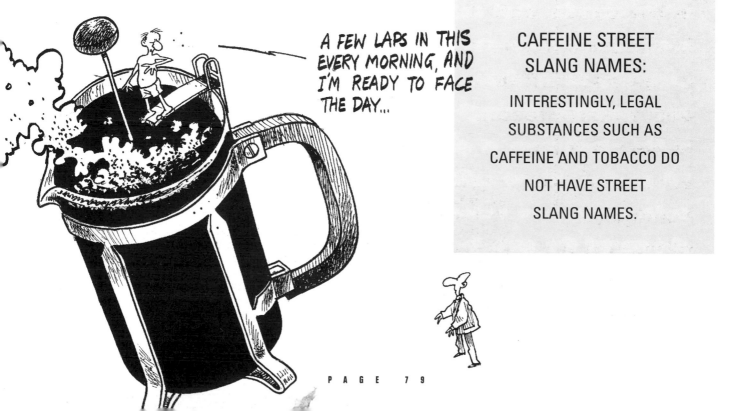

A FEW LAPS IN THIS EVERY MORNING, AND I'M READY TO FACE THE DAY...

CAFFEINE STREET SLANG NAMES:

INTERESTINGLY, LEGAL SUBSTANCES SUCH AS CAFFEINE AND TOBACCO DO NOT HAVE STREET SLANG NAMES.

DRUG INFORMATION CHAPTER 20

Cocaine

COCAINE is an intelligence test. If you take it you fail.
Paul Kantner, Jefferson Starship

Cocaine or 'coke' is the name given to the white powder that movie moguls and rock stars poured carefully on to sheets of glass and 'snorted' through straws in the cloakroom at glittering LA parties. Many called it quits when they sneezed and showered the powder and portions of their nasal septum clear across the room.

SOURCE:
The South American coca bush, which is indigenous to the eastern slopes of the Andes mountains, mainly in Peru and Bolivia.

HISTORY:
Coca leaves have been chewed for centuries by the Andean Indians.

NEUROTRANSMITTERS DEPLETED:
Adrenalin, noradrenalin, dopamine.

BODY SITES AFFECTED:
Arterial blood vessels, heart, adrenal glands, mucosal membranes.

INITIAL MOOD ALTERATION:
Improves mood, enhances alertness, suppresses appetite, heightens excitement.

ACUTE SIDE EFFECTS:
Racing pulse, high blood pressure, ruptured blood vessels, heart attacks, strokes.

CHRONIC SIDE EFFECTS:
Rotting of nasal septum, addiction, respiratory disorders, anxiety and depression, possible psychosis, circulatory disorders, heart disease, epilepsy, diabetes.

For many centuries coca leaves mixed with lime have been chewed by Andean Indians to relieve hunger and fatigue. During the Incan empire, coca was used by priests and nobles to aid the quest for religious truths and to signify membership of the aristocracy. It is estimated that 90 percent of the adult male Andean Indian population still regularly chew coca leaves. The Spanish, who invaded Peru in 1533, were impressed with coca and encouraged its use by their Indian slaves, who worked in goldmines at high altitudes and in extreme cold.

When coca leaves began entering Europe in substantial quantities in the 1800s, they formed the basis for a number of popular tonics. Coca lozenges and coca tea were recommended for common complaints such as sore throats and headaches.

In 1860 the German chemist Albert Niemann extracted pure cocaine from coca leaves. In 1884 a young Viennese neurologist called Sigmund Freud (yes, that Sigmund Freud) tested cocaine on himself and enthused rapturously over its stimulant properties. It was his considered opinion that the exhilaration and euphoria produced by cocaine was less harmful than the effects of alcohol.

For a period, cocaine was widely prescribed for the relief of anxiety and depression. Across the Atlantic, a Georgia pharmacist called John Pemberton was working on a medication based on extracts from the coca leaf and the kola nut. The former contained cocaine and the latter caffeine. Pemberton's Coca-Cola (yes, that Coca-Cola) was sold as the 'intellectual beverage and temperance

drink' and understandably proved very popular. When the disastrous consequences of cocaine abuse became known, it ceased to be prescribed as a medicine and vanished from Coca-Cola, which survived very well without it.

Cocaine is extracted from the coca leaves as a coarse salt; these crystals or 'rocks' range from 60 to 99 percent pure. After further refining it is sold on the street as a fine white crystalline powder, commonly known as 'coke' or 'snow'. The purity varies. Frequently it is diluted with inert substances such as starch, talcum powder and sugar, or with psychoactive drugs that share some of its actions, such as amphetamines.

In the Western world cocaine is commonly admin-istered by inhalation through the nostrils. During the 1980s, a smokeable form known as 'freebase' or 'crack' was developed. It looks like brownish clumps of sugar and tends to make a crackling sound when smoked.

Whether smoked, sniffed or injected, cocaine has an immediate effect on the whole body. It acts as a local anaesthetic and as a powerful general stimulant on the brain. It does this by mimicking the natural adrenalin response of the body to stress.

Adrenalin is the chemical released into the bloodstream when you go on a terrifying roller coaster ride. If the ride isn't terrifying, the body doesn't release adrenalin and the thrill-seeker is denied the natural 'rush'. Cocaine can provide a similar 'rush' in the privacy of your own bathroom.

It is a powerful vasoconstrictor – the narrowing of blood vessels in the nose and throat interferes with the oxygen supply to nerve endings, producing immediate anaesthesia. Sniffers' mucous membranes are numbed, and repeated use causes widespread cell damage and the eventual rotting of the nasal septum.

In the brain, cocaine works by draining the synaptic tanks of the neurotransmitters noradrenalin, dopamine and adrenalin. The rapid spilling of these transmitters causes the 'rush' associated with cocaine use. The nerve pathways served by these transmitters regulate muscle tone, facilitate mental energy, heighten attention span, suppress appetite and intensify pleasure.

Because cocaine is rapidly metabolised by the liver, the rush is short-lived, encouraging the user to try again. With frequent use the brain depletes the supply of these transmitters and the user has to take larger and larger amounts to duplicate the initial rush. Regular users only appreciate how powerful this depletion is when they try to stop taking it. This is the basis of addiction.

Aside from transmitter interference, cocaine's vasoconstrictor properties reduce the flow of blood through the brain. Scans of regular users show long-term deterioration in brain metabolism.

Cocaine also acts as a direct stimulant on the heart and the adrenal cortex, triggering the release of adrenalin into the bloodstream. The pulse rate shoots up and blood pressure increases steeply – the typical 'fight or flight' response.

The surge of extra blood into a system where capacity has been severely reduced due to the narrowing of blood vessels puts dangerous pressure on the arterial walls. These vessels can burst in the brain, causing cardiac arrest and/or respiratory failure.

Cocaine passes easily across mucous membranes into the bloodstream and brain. In pregnant women it crosses the placental barrier and starves the developing foetus of life-supporting blood flow. Pregnant women using cocaine have a very high incidence of miscarriage – 38 percent more than normal – and of premature birth. Cocaine babies are three times more likely to die from cot death than babies born to heroin addicts.

COCAINE STREET SLANG NAMES.

BIG C, BLOW, BOMBITA, BERNIES, 'C', CHARLES, CHARLIE, COKE, DREAM, DUST, FLAKE, FLY, GOLD-DUST, HEAVEN, HER, ICE, SNOW, NOSE CANDY, POISON, SCHOOLBOY, STARDUST, SUGAR AND WHITE LADY, AMONG OTHERS.

'Cocaine is God's way of telling you that you have too much money.'

STING

Hallucinogens

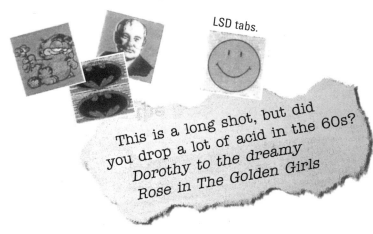

LSD tabs.

This is a long shot, but did you drop a lot of acid in the 60s? Dorothy to the dreamy Rose in The Golden Girls

An hallucination is a sensory experience with no basis in external reality. Sitting in a theatre watching a magician saw a beautiful assistant in half is to witness an illusion. Sitting at home staring at the wallpaper and seeing a magician saw a beautiful assistant in half is to experience an hallucination.

SOURCE:
Hallucinogens occur naturally in a wide variety of plants, as well as in some fish and toads. Synthetic hallucinogens are easily manufactured in the laboratory.

HISTORY:
Naturally occurring hallucinogens have been used as folk medicines and in religious ceremonies for thousands of years.

NEUROTRANSMITTERS DEPLETED:
Serotonin, acetylcholine, noradrenalin.

INITIAL MOOD ALTERATION:
Hallucinations, which can be rapturous or terrifying, depending on the circumstances.

ACUTE SIDE EFFECTS:
Headaches, blurred vision and nausea are possible, as are dizziness and convulsions.

CHRONIC SIDE EFFECTS:
Flashbacks are common, and permanent psychosis or schizophrenia is possible.

Norse tribesman used the mushroom Amanita muscaria to trigger rage before going into battle. The word 'berserk' comes from the bearskin jackets the Vikings wore while raping, looting and pillaging.

An hallucinogen is any substance that causes hallucinations. Most of the drugs that distort sensory experience resemble certain neurotransmitters closely enough to attach to their receptors. The hallucinogenic drugs resemble the neurotransmitters noradrenalin, serotonin and, less commonly, acetylcholine.

'Two hours after taking the drug, I felt I had been under its influence for thousands of years. The remainder of my life on planet earth seemed to stretch ahead into infinity, and at the same time I felt infinitely old…

'Boundaries between self and nonself evaporate, giving rise to a serene sense of being at one with the universe. I recall muttering to myself "All is one, all is one"…

'This was followed by a loss of awareness of just who I was. I began to call out "Who am I? Where is the world?" At the height of this disintegration, I was terrified. I tried frantically to remember my name – hoping thus to recapture reality – but it eluded me. In the end I grasped at the one name I could think of – "San Francisco." I repeated it again and again. "San Francisco, San Francisco, San Francisco." '

Solomon H Snyder describing an LSD trip in his book **Drugs and the Brain.**

The 'magic mushrooms' of Mexico and Central America have a longer history of human use than any other mind-altering plant. Stone sculptures of psychoactive mushrooms found in El Salvador, Guatemala and parts of Mexico date back well before 500 BC. The faces of gods carved on the stems confirm the mushroom's role in religious ritual. Teonanactl, the Indian name for one kind of mushroom, means 'food of the gods'.

The Aztec Indians of Mexico used peyote cactus, which contains mescaline, on religious and ceremonial occasions. Peyote use was incorporated into Christianity by Mexicans and some American Indians, who still consume it in religious rituals today.

Hallucinogens are found in many botanical species and in the salivary glands of some species of frog. In the South Pacific there is an hallucinogenic fish. The hallucinogens atropine and scopolamine are found in the plants belladonna  (deadly nightshade), datura, nutmeg, mace and morning glory seeds. Atropine and scopolamine are structurally similar to the neurotransmitter acetylcholine.

The botanical hallucinogens are easily synthesised and an almost endless number of new hallucinogens have been created in the laboratory, including LSD, which is the yardstick by which all the other synthetic hallucinogens – such as DMT, MDMA (ecstasy), MDA, DOM (STP) and PCP (angel dust) are measured.

LSD was synthesised in 1938 when the Swiss chemist Albert Hoffman, working in the Sandoz laboratories at Basel, combined diethylamide with lysergic acid, a non-hallucinogenic substance derived from fungus. He was unaware of its mind-altering properties until he accidentally ingested some of it in 1943 and experienced the world's first LSD trip. By his own account it was not a particularly pleasant experience:

'Pieces of furniture assumed grotesque threatening forms…A demon had invaded me, taken possession of my body, mind and soul…I was seized by the dreadful fear I was going insane…I was taken to another world, another place, another time…Was I dying?'

Reports on LSD first appeared in science journals in 1947. Some researchers wondered if it had a role to play in the treatment of mental illness. In the 1950s, Sandoz distributed the drug to scientists around the world for the purposes of biochemical and animal behaviour research. In the US, military intelligence conducted clandestine research into hallucinogenics as possible agents for psychological and chemical warfare.

In the 'psychedelic' 1960s, illegal LSD production reached epidemic proportions. Encouraged by LSD gurus such as Harvard psychologist Timothy Leary and the novelists Aldous Huxley and William Burroughs, many thousands of young people seeking mind expansion and the keys to the universe eagerly dropped acid.

While there are no reported cases of anyone dying from an LSD overdose, there are numerous reports of people leaping to their deaths from tall buildings, and psychiatric wards around the world still shelter ageing hippies with LSD-induced schizophrenia. LSD's potential for inducing psychotic states in abusers led to its prohibition in the late 60s.

LSD works by interfering with the brain's ability to selectively store immediate experiences. As a result, the cortex is overwhelmed with sensory input. This flooding of information that you are experiencing, storing and comparing with past experiences – this condition where one thought reminds you of a million others, where one colour splits into a million other colours, where if you smell a turkey you can see a turkey – is believed to be the basis of the psychedelic experience.

LSD is readily absorbed from the gastro-intestinal tract, metabolised in the liver and excreted in the bile.

Like most other drugs, it affects individuals differently, depending on the amount taken, the age and experience of the user, the method of use and whether it is used in conjunction with other drugs. Differences in composition, purity and strength make the impact and duration of the effect on the user highly unpredictable.

In low doses, LSD can alter mood and perception without always producing an hallucination. Moods can swing from elation to depression. Perceptual changes can be pleasant or unpleasant. In higher doses the drug produces hallucinations that can be short- or long-acting and, in some instances, recurring events – experienced weeks, even months later – called 'flashbacks'.

With low doses, the user is generally aware that they are experiencing a fraudulent reality. At higher doses the user can lose all sense of reality. This state usually passes but, tragically, some users can become permanently psychotic, either from the stress of a 'bad trip' or from a schizophrenic reaction. Some 'bad trips' can result in terrifyingly aggressive behaviour, self-mutilation, homicide and suicide.

LSD use can trigger adverse physical side effects such as headache, blurred vision, overwhelming tiredness, nausea, poor appetite, increased blood pressure, faster or slower heartbeat, dizziness, trembling and occasionally convulsions.

Some research suggests that it increases the risk of spontaneous abortion.

While there is no evidence of physical dependence, regular users can become psychologically dependent on the drug – in preference to the humdrum pressures of the real world they get off on escaping into a psychedelic universe. Other users sometimes can't get back to planet earth fast enough.

HALLUCINOGENS STREET SLANG NAMES.

LSD, ACID, BARRELS, BEAST, BIG D,

BLOTTERS, DOTS, BLUE ACID, BLUE MIST,

BLUE HEAVEN, CAP, CHOCOLATE CHIPS,

'D', DOMES, FLASH, GHOST, HAWK, HAZE,

'L', LYSERGIDE, MELLOW YELLOWS,

MICRODOTS, PEACE, PEARLY GATES,

TABS, TICKET, TRIPS, WHITE LIGHTNING,

WINDOWPANE, GARFIELD, SNOOPY,

DONALD DUCK, MICKEY MOUSE, DUST,

HOG, PCP, BUTTONS, CACTUS, 'P', ROCKET

FUEL, SHROOMS, MAGIC MUSHROOMS

AND SACRED MUSHROOMS.

THE ECSTASY AND THE AGONY

In the mid-eighties in the United States there came whisper of a new wonder drug which could ease all of life's emotional ills, open windows of enlightenment, enhance feelings of love and well-being and, given half a chance, raise the dead. Claims about this new wonder drug were reminiscent of the virtues ascribed to LSD in the 1960s (since proven to be false), namely that it helped people trust one another and broke down barriers between therapists and patients, lovers, and other family members. This magical elixir was called 'ecstasy' – XTC, doves or biscuits on the streets.

The medical and scientific community, and the black-market chemists who manufacture it, know it by its scientific abbreviation MDMA, which is short for 3-4methylenedioxymethamphetmine. On noisy dance floors, '3-4methylenedioxymethamphetamine' is a bit of a mouthful so it's entirely understandable that 'ecstasy' is the preferred *nom de plume*.

Ecstasy is one of a whole new breed of substances dubbed 'designer drugs'. Designer drugs are synthetic chemical compounds manufactured in laboratories. They are analogues of other drugs of abuse that is, they are cousins rather than clones of the original

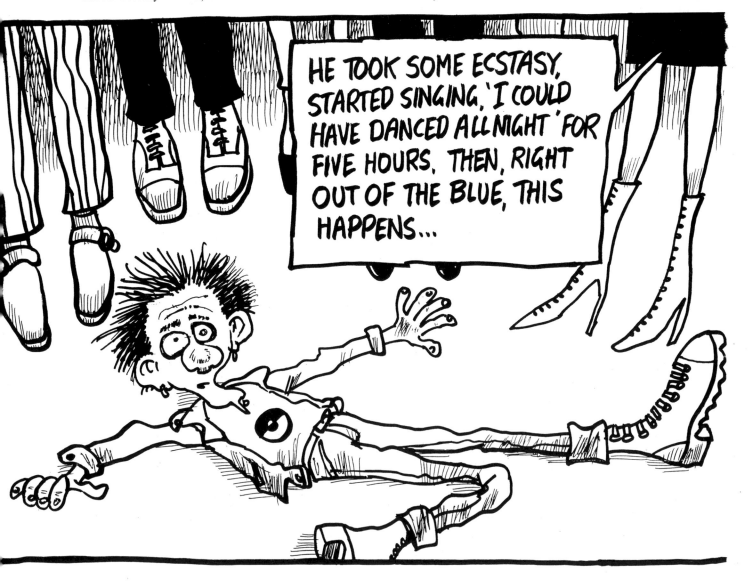

drug. They are similar in effect to the drug they are intended to mimic, but they differ slightly in structure. These slight structural differences can have a profound impact on potency, which is what the black-market chemists were seeking in the first place, and designer drugs can be considerably more dangerous than the original drug of abuse. The street names of designer drugs vary according to time, place and manufacture. And these names change frequently.

MDMA is a modification of another designer drug, the hallucinogenic amphetamine MDA – methylenedioxyamphetamine, which is also known by the street name 'love drug'. MDA was a popular drug of abuse in the 1960s because it produced a heightened need to for users to talk to and be with other people. It became fashionable on American campuses in the 1980s, and was favoured as a therapeutic tool by some psychiatrists, until research scientists found that MDA damaged serotonin neurones in the brain, and it was classified as a Class A drug.

Because MDMA is structurally similar to both methamphetamine and mescaline, it has some of the stimulant properties of the former and some of the hallucinogenic properties of the latter. Originally synthesised in 1914 as an appetite suppressant, it was never manufactures because it also caused nausea. It's one thing to avoid food, it's another thing to projectile vomit food across the room, so it disappeared from view until 1972, when a group of Californian entrepreneurs decided to manufacture it illegally. Bay making extravagant claims on its behalf they had, by the 1980s, created an illicit market for it worth many millions of dollars.

At the height of the first ecstasy boom in the USA and Canada, emergency rooms and drug abuse clinics reported numerous MDMA-related crises involving severe anxiety reactions, paranoia and depression. In 1985, MDMA was classified as a Class A drug, and its manufacture and trafficking became a serious criminal offence, but despite this there has been an international re-emergence of ecstasy.

Ecstasy users encounter many problems similar to those found with the use of amphetamines and cocaine. Psychological difficulties include confusion, depression, sleep problems, drug craving, severe anxiety, possible psychosis and, in conjunction with other drugs, suicidal thoughts. Physical symptoms include muscle tension, involuntary teeth-clenching, nausea, blurred vision, rapid eye movements, faintness and chills or sweating. Increases in heart rate and blood pressure are an additional risk for people with circulatory or heart disease.

Because MDMA is manufactured in illegal laboratories, its synthesis is not subject to regulation or control, and users can never be certain that what they are purchasing is free of contaminants. Some contaminants, such as strychnine, can be added deliberately to prolong the duration of MDMA's effects.

The morning after a night out on ecstasy, users commonly suffer from extreme exhaustion, they are dehydrated, and their breathing can become slow and laboured. The American satirist, P. J. O'Rourke, writing in Rolling Stone about the after-effects of an XTC trip, said, 'On the second day, all the effects were gone, but I was tired and depressed, "X" lag is pretty substantial for such a toy flip-out. A long run for a short slide. TUNE IN, TURN ON, GO TO THE OFFICE LATE ON MONDAY.'

ECSTASY
STREET SLANG NAMES.
E, XTC, DOVES, DISCO BISCUITS, ECHOES, ECCIES, BURGERS, FANTASY, HUG DRUG.

Inhalants

'Anyone got a match?'
Famous last words
of many solvent
sniffers

Apart from ether and nitrous oxide (laughing gas, which is used in anaesthesia and misused by a handful of doctors seeking escape at the end of a long day), it is difficult to think of inhalants as drugs, because most of them were never intended to be used that way.

SOURCE:
Synthetic chemicals used widely in transport and industry.

HISTORY:
Solvent abuse is a recent phenomenon.

NEUROTRANSMITTERS DEPLETED:
GABA.

BRAIN SITE AFFECTED:
Cortex and breathing centre in brain stem.

INITIAL MOOD ALTERATION:
Euphoria, intoxication, drowsiness.

ACUTE SIDE EFFECTS:
Constant sniffing, sneezing, nosebleeds, runny nose, runny eyes, excess salivation, foul breath, nausea, listlessness.

CHRONIC SIDE EFFECTS:
Addiction, physical debilitation, impaired judgment, altered personality, metabolic poisoning from contaminants.

IT'S HIS OWN INVENTION. IT CONTAINS ENOUGH SOLVENT FOR A FOUR DAY HIGH. IT PROVIDES SHELTER AND WHEN THE COPS COME FOR HIS REMAINS THEY'RE ALREADY IN A BODY BAG.

Who would have thought, for instance, that the gas inside ping-pong balls was worth a sniff? Or that typists' Tippex had another use beyond correcting spelling mistakes? To most people, you would have to be out of your mind to breathe in petrol fumes, and if you weren't to begin with, you would be later. *But some young people do.*

Inhalant abuse by children and adolescents is a small but extremely serious problem in many countries.

Solvents enter the bloodstream through the lungs without first passing through the liver, where they might have stood some chance of being detoxified before rampaging through the rest of the body.

Because they were never intended for human consumption, many solvents contain metabolic poisons, such as the heavy metal lead, and known carcinogens, such as benzanthracene, which cause cancer.

Glue and petrol are the most commonly abused inhalants. Many solvent products such as the alcohols – methanol, propanol, butanol – are hydrocarbons that reduce the oxygen supply to the brain by depressing the respiratory centre in much the same fashion as their less toxic cousin ethanol.

First comes euphoria, then sedation, drowsiness, sleep, anaesthesia, coma and death.

Unless you've got an intravenous drip filled with ethanol, alcohol consumption requires some active participation on the part of the drinker. Raising the elbow is a central part of the whole operation. But the solvent abuser – merely by attaching a plastic bag filled with inhalant over their head – can passively go the full distance to coma and death.

This doesn't stop young solvent abusers from believing themselves indestructible. Group sniffing of volatile substances over several hours in poorly

ventilated areas can prove fatal if just one of the group grabs a cigarette and absent-mindedly strikes a match. The authors consider that young solvent abusers are better off left in a well-ventilated park.

The signs of solvent abuse include constant sniffing, sneezing, nosebleeds, coughing, running eyes and nose, surface burn marks below the eyes, nausea, loss of appetite, excess salivation, foul breath, general debilitation, lack of physical coordination and impaired judgment.

Repeated sniffing of concentrated vapours over time permanently damages the central nervous system and alters the personality.

INHALANTS
STREET SLANG NAMES.

POPPERS, RUSH, LOCKER-ROOM,

LAUGHING GAS, SNAPPERS,

BENZENE, 'G' AND 'P'.

Marijuana

Keep off the grass City Council sign.

Unique to *Cannabis sativa* are the resinous substances found in the stem, leaf and flowerheads – the 62 cannabinoids. The most active, the most studied, and the one that occurs in the highest concentration is the psychoactive agent Delta-9-tetrahydrocannabinol (THC).

SOURCE: *Cannabis sativa* plant.

HISTORY: In ancient times cannabis fibre was used to make clothing and rope. For many centuries in Asia, the Middle East and North Africa, cannabis was used widely as a medicine, as well as for its psychoactive properties.

NEUROTRANSMITTERS DEPLETED: Acetylcholine, serotonin, endorphins and GABA.

INITIAL MOOD ALTERATION: Mild euphoria, relaxation, time distortion, intensification of ordinary sensory experience.

ACUTE SIDE EFFECTS: Reddening of the whites of the eyes, dry throat, elevated appetite, and anxiety, panic and paranoia, especially in naive users. Short-term memory impairment. Concentration span impairment. Psychomotor impairment. Increased risk of an accident if you drive a motor vehicle or operate machinery when stoned. Possible psychotic symptoms such as delusions and hallucinations.

CHRONIC SIDE EFFECTS: Probable respiratory diseases. Possible cannabis addiction. Memory damage and decline in other intellectual skills. Increased risk of cancers of aerodigestive tract. Increased risk of developing schizophrenia. Increased risk of leukaemia in offspring exposed while in the womb. Possible chromosome damage. Increased risk of birth defects in children of women who use cannabis during pregnancy. A marked decline in occupational performance in adults, and educational under-achievement in children. Reduced production of reproductive hormones. Impaired ovulation, sperm production and libido. Reduced white blood cell production and impaired immune system.

Why cannabis produces so many psychoactive agents near the surface of its leaves, stems and flowerheads is not clear, but they are believed to serve a role in moisture retention.

The concentration of THC varies between the three common forms of cannabis available on the market – marijuana, hashish and hash oil. Given that users may mix all three forms together, trying to compute the strength of an average dose is a thankless task. All that can be said with any certainty is that over the past 30 years the selective breeding of hybrid varieties of *Cannabis sativa* has increased THC concentrations in the leaf and flowerhead to the point where today's joint could be between five and 50 times more potent than its 1960s predecessor.

Taken orally – i.e., other than by smoking – THC may take over an hour to enter the bloodstream, but it is more potent and longer-acting that way. Upon inhalation THC is absorbed from the lungs and enters the bloodstream in minutes. The initial metabolism of it takes place in the lungs, followed by more extensive metabolism in the liver, transforming THC to a number of even more active metabolites detectable in blood plasma and urine.

Because THC is fat-soluble, it can accumulate in body lipids, which are a structural component of every cell membrane in the body. Consequently, THC may be active in the nervous system long after it is no longer detectable in the blood. It has a half-life of several days in fat. It takes weeks to completely eliminate from the body all the THC from a single joint. Of particular concern is the storage of THC in the lipid-rich testes and brain.

BLOCKING CELLULAR DRAINS

THC's fat-solubility allows it to move easily into the lipo-protein membranes surrounding every cell in the body. In pregnant women, it slips through the placental barrier into the foetal bloodstream. Likewise in breastfeeding mothers, THC crosses easily into breast milk.

In high concentrations, THC molecules clog cell membranes, making it difficult for nutrients to cross in and for other substances to move out. The same membranes surround the nucleus – the genetic library of the cell. They cover the surface of mitochondria – the cell's power stations. They line the walls of the tiny canals that thread through the endoplasmic reticulum – the cell's light industrial zones that manufacture enzymes, proteins and hormones.

The clogging of all these membranes lowers cellular metabolic efficiency.

In 1990, Herkenham and his colleagues localised specific cannabinoid receptors in the brain. These receptors are particularly dense in the frontal cortex, the hippocampus and the cerebellum.

The **FRONTAL CORTEX** is the place where incoming sensory information is processed and voluntary (conscious) motor activity is initiated.

The **HIPPOCAMPUS** is where incoming sensory experiences are converted into short-term memory, which in turn is consolidated into permanent memory.

The **CEREBELLUM** is where proprioception (the body's understanding of where it is positioned in space), equilibrium (balance control) and motor activity (voluntary and involuntary movement) are coordinated.

Because of its cellular staying power, THC is similar to sunburn – sunburn does not go away when the sun sets.

DR ROBERT GILKESON

In 1992, Devane and colleagues identified a brain molecule that binds to the cannabinoid receptors. The molecule, which is mimicked by THC, is also fat-soluble. It has been named 'anandamide', from the Sanskrit word for bliss.

In 1988, Howlett and his colleagues found that cannabinoids inhibit the enzyme that synthesises cyclic AMP. Neurotransmitters pass messages between cells, and within those cells the same messages are passed on by a host of secondary messengers, the most important of which is cyclic AMP. Disruption of the secondary messenger network is believed to be the basis for THC's wide-ranging effects.

Herkenham's studies of THC receptor distribution in the cerebellum were confirmed by Volkov et al in 1991 using Pet (positron emission tomography) scans – in other words, brain mapping. Thanks to these scans, scientists can now 'visualise' what is actually happening to the brain while it goes about its daily business. Volkov's tests showed that chronic marijuana users had a decreased cerebellar metabolism, which could account for THC's disruption of proprioception and motor coordination.

While Pet scans are invaluable in measuring the uptake of glucose (the fuel on which the brain runs) in the cortex and cerebellum, which form the outer layers of the brain, they currently lack the resolution to measure the metabolic activity of structures such as the hippocampus, which are buried deep in the human brain. To measure the effect of THC on the hippocampus scientists have had to conduct post-mortem, electron-microscope studies of monkeys and rats exposed to marijuana smoke.

In 1987 Scallet et al reported a staggering 44 percent reduction in the number of synapses, and a significant decrease in the neuronal volume of the hippocampus, in rats given THC orally for 90 days. Campbell et al in 1986 reported that THC suppresses hippocampal electrical activity in rats.

MARIJUANA AND MEMORY

Schwartz et al in a 1989 American study reported the results of an exceptionally well-controlled test of persistent short-term memory impairment in a group of marijuana-smoking middle-class adolescents.

Their median age was 16, and they had at least eight years of formal education. Their performance was compared with that of a group of controls matched for age and IQ. When initially tested, the cannabis-dependent boys and girls did much worse on short-term memory tests than the control group, and after six weeks of supervised abstention from intoxicants they still presented short-term memory deficits. The Schwartz study proves the specific lasting power of marijuana to impair memory storage, a critical part of the learning process.

MARIJUANA AND PSYCHOMOTOR PERFORMANCE

The most striking evidence of the lingering disruption of marijuana on memory and coordination was provided in 1991 by investigators who recruited 10 experienced private pilots for a double-blind experiment. The subjects were trained for eight hours on a computerised flight simulator. The test started one morning with a control 'flight', after which each subject smoked either a marijuana cigarette containing 19 milligrams of THC or a placebo cigarette from which the THC had been removed. The simulated landing was repeated one, four and 24 hours later.

In every case, the worst performance occurred one hour after THC inhalation. Even 24 hours later, pilots who had smoked marijuana still experienced significant difficulty in aligning the computer-generated plane on the centre of the runway. The pilots themselves, however (none of whom, of course, knew which kind of cigarette they'd smoked), reported no awareness of marijuana after-effects on their performance, mood or alertness.

MARIJUANA AND ROAD ACCIDENTS

A 1990 US National Transportation Safety Board study of 182 road accidents involving 86 trucks in which 210 people were killed found that a third of the victims, whose bodies were examined, had recently used some substance of abuse – 12.8 percent had used marijuana, 12.5 alcohol and 8.5 cocaine.

MARIJUANA AND SCHIZOPHRENIA

A 15-year Swedish study involving 55,000 military conscripts showed that heavy cannabis users were six times more likely than non-users to develop schizophrenia. Clinicians report that the symptoms of cannabis toxic psychosis resemble the symptoms of schizophrenia.

MARIJUANA EFFECTS ON HUMAN GROWTH

Nobel prizewinner Dr Julius Axelrod found that the mitotic index of marijuana users is less than half that of non-users – 2.3 percent compared to 5.9. The mitotic index (the percentage of body cells being divided at any given moment) is a measure of the body's ability to grow and repair itself. In a mature adult, rapid cell division includes sperm production in men, the formation of new gut lining and the bone marrow production of red and white blood cells.

In gestation, infancy and puberty, rapid cell division occurs in all body systems. When one cell does not divide properly it is a small tragedy; when billions of cells do not divide properly it is a biological catastrophe.

In 1987, a Jamaican study using high-speed computer voice analysis studies showed that infants born to marijuana-smoking mothers had a much higher incidence of voice anomaly than did the infants of mothers who did not smoke marijuana. In 1989, another study found that infants born to marijuana-smoking mothers were shorter, weighed less and had smaller head circumferences at birth.

In a study published in 1990 on the long-term developmental and behavioural effects from intrauterine marijuana exposure, Freid et al found that even four years later children exposed to THC in the womb scored significantly lower in verbal and memory tests.

In 1989, Robinson et al reported a tenfold increase in the incidence of leukaemia in the children of mothers who had smoked marijuana just before or during pregnancy.

MARIJUANA AND RESPIRATORY TRACT CANCER

Marijuana smoke contains gases and tiny particles. The gases include the known carcinogens vinyl chloride, dimethyl and methylethyl nitrosamines in roughly the same amounts as in tobacco smoke. The particles include the known carcinogens benzanthracene and benzopyrene in nearly double the concentrations found in tobacco smoke. People smoke marijuana far less frequently than cigarettes, but joints are seldom filtered and the smoke is inhaled more deeply into their lungs and held there longer.

Tashkin et al, in a 1980 study of young marijuana smokers, found symptoms of airway obstruction. In another 1980 study, Tennant et al examined bronchial biopsies of chronic marijuana users and found squamous cell hyperplasia – a known precursor of lung cancer in tobacco smokers.

MARIJUANA AND AGEING

Recent studies of the hippocampus in rats by Landfield and Eldridge suggest a possible mechanism by which THC accelerates brain ageing. The steroid hormones released by the adrenal glands in response to stress – the glucocorticoids – are known to accelerate ageing. Pacific salmon, for example, die from the destructive metabolic consequences of elevated glucocorticoid secretion after spawning. They grow old and die in a matter of days.

The hippocampus is rich in glucocorticoid receptors, which makes it particularly vulnerable to brain ageing of the Alzheimer's type. THC is structurally similar to the glucocorticoid hormones and has been shown to bind with the glucocorticoid receptors in the hippocampus of rats, and with prolonged exposure THC decreases neuron size and number.

HEY- I'M UNEMPLOYED. I HAVE NO SKILLS, I'M FROM A DYSFUNCTIONAL FAMILY, SO I SMOKE FOUR JOINTS A DAY... - WHAT ELSE HAVE I GOT TO LOOK FORWARD TO?

FOUR JOINTS A DAY HUH... NOT A LOT REALLY...

MARIJUANA
STREET SLANG NAMES.

POT, GRASS, WEED, DOPE,

MARY JANE, ELECTRIC PUHA,

SINSEMILLA, BLOW, DRAW, REEFER,

PUFF, HOOCH, BULLET, STASH, HASH,

HASH O, CABBAGE, NUMBER,

GANJA, GUNJA, HAY, ACAPULCO GOLD,

ACE, AFRICAN BLACK, AUNT MARY,

BABY, BALE, BOMB, BRICK, HEMP, J,

JANE, KILLER, KILLER WEED,

MARY WARNER, ROACH, SHIT, TEA,

TWIST AND WACKY BACCY.

Nicotine

> People who don't smoke have a terrible time finding something polite to do with their lips.
> P.J. O'Rourke

Nicotine is a powerful stimulant and works by mimicking the effect of the neurotransmitter acetylcholine, and to a lesser extent the transmitters serotonin and GABA.

SOURCE:
Nicotine is an alkaloid found in the leaves of the tobacco plant *Nicotiana tabacum.*

HISTORY:
Both the plant and its most potent ingredient were named in honour of Jean Nicot, French ambassador to Portugal in the 1560s. Nicot was an ardent publicist of the plant's medical and other virtues during the decades following the discovery of its use among tribes of North and Central America by early Western explorers.

NEUROTRANSMITTERS DEPLETED:
Acetylcholine, serotonin, GABA.

INITIAL MOOD ALTERATION:
Nicotine acts as a stimulant, increasing intellectual alertness.

ACUTE SIDE EFFECTS:
Raises heart rate.

CHRONIC SIDE EFFECTS:
Addiction, premature ageing of the skin, circulatory disorders, heart disease, respiratory disorders, possible lung cancer when smoked with tobacco.

PASSIVE SMOKING BIG KILLER IN STATES

It increases heart rate, arouses parts of the cerebral cortex, contracts skeletal muscles and modifies behaviour by directly stimulating certain receptors that normally respond to acetylcholine.

Considered more addictive than heroin, it is an extremely toxic substance. Two or three drops of the pure alkaloid on the tongue will rapidly kill an adult. A typical cigarette contains 15–20 mg of nicotine. When smoked, less than 1 mg enters the bloodstream and reaches the brain.

Tar is the name given to the particulate matter in cigarette smoke. Many of the constituents of tar are known to cause cancer. Someone smoking 20 cigarettes a day deposits 120 g of tar in their lungs over the course of a single year.

Cigarette smoke also contains the colourless, odourless gas carbon monoxide (CO). A product of incomplete combustion, it is the poisonous component in automobile engine exhaust fumes. In the blood, it binds with haemoglobin, preventing red blood cells from carrying oxygen. In high concentrations it literally suffocates the blood system by blocking its oxygen-carrying capacity. The localised lack of oxygen can damage artery walls, initiating the development of arterio-sclerotic plaque.

Cigarette smokers are 10 times more likely than non-smokers to develop lung cancer and respiratory tract diseases such as bronchitis and emphysema. Cigarette smokers are three times more likely to die at an early age from a heart attack.

Cigarette smoking in the developed countries is the leading cause of death among young adults.

Nicotine also constricts small arteries, which means that smokers are more likely to suffer from circulatory disorders and from stomach ulcers that heal only slowly. Skin wounds also tend to heal slowly. Smoking depletes vitamin C levels and smokers appear to have less effective immune systems than non-smokers.

Women who smoke have smaller babies and many more premature births, miscarriages and stillbirths. In addition, there is evidence of impairment in the mental and physical development of their children. Women smokers tend to reach menopause at an earlier age.

Cigarette smoking prematurely ages the skin of the face.

Children and adolescents who have learned to cope with the initial un-pleasantness of cigarette smoke are better able to handle the harshness of marijuana smoke. In that sense, tobacco acts as a gateway drug for marijuana.

Surveys conducted in Britain in 1990 showed that 50 percent of tobacco smokers had also tried an illegal drug, compared with only two percent of non-smokers. Which proves that once you have lost your pharmaceutical virginity, it's that much easier to get into bed with another substance of abuse.

ANOTHER VICIOUS ATTACK ON THE LIBERTY OF THE INDIVIDUAL...

Opiates/Narcotics

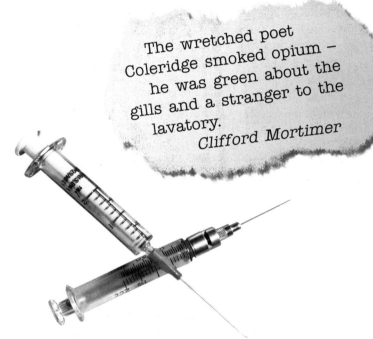

The wretched poet Coleridge smoked opium – he was green about the gills and a stranger to the lavatory.
Clifford Mortimer

SOURCE:
The poppy plant.

HISTORY:
Opium from poppy plants has been used by humans for more than 7000 years.

NEUROTRANSMITTERS DEPLETED:
Endorphins.

BRAIN SITES AFFECTED:
Cortex, brain stem and spinal cord.

INITIAL MOOD ALTERATION:
Euphoria, serenity, analgesia.

ACUTE SIDE EFFECTS:
Vomiting, constipation, reduced sex drive, itching. Death from overdose.

CHRONIC SIDE EFFECTS:
Shrunken gums, apathy, addiction. possibility of blood poisoning, arterial ulcerations. Risk of Hepatitis A, B & C and blood-transmitted diseases, including AIDS, from sharing needles and using dirty needles.

Opiates, or narcotics, are brain depressants with analgesic (painkilling) and sedative (calming) properties. They include opium and its derivatives heroin, morphine and codeine, plus the synthetic substances demerol and methadone.

OPIUM is the brownish gum made by drying the juice extracted from the unripe seed pods of the Oriental poppy *Papaver somniferum*.

The painkilling and bliss-out properties of opium and its derivatives make it a wonderfully useful medical tool. They also make it a substance with a huge potential for abuse, crime and corruption.

The first mention of opium use is found in Assyrian medical texts dating back to 5000 BC. In 1500 BC Egyptian physicians used it as an anaesthetic, and in the seventh century AD the opium poppy was brought into China from the Middle East and India.

In 1541 the Swiss alchemist Paracelsus dissolved opium in alcohol and dispensed it as a tincture called laudanum. This was used extensively as a pain reliever, cough suppressant and sedative, and also for the control of dysentery.

In the seventeenth and eighteenth centuries, opium abuse reached epidemic proportions in many countries. But Chinese government attempts to control its importation, sale and use were vigorously opposed by the British because they interfered with their profitable trade in the opium grown in their prize colony, India. This led to the opium war of

1839–42. The British won, and opium cultivation and importation were again made legal in China. Subsequently, Chinese emigrants carried the habit of opium-smoking to the rest of the world. Many countries eventually banned its general use, though it was used as a standard medical drug right through until the nineteenth century.

MORPHINE – named after the Greek God of dreams, Morpheus – was isolated from opium in 1803. It quickly proved an even more effective painkiller than opium, and use of the parent compound steadily declined. The invention of the hypodermic syringe in 1853 allowed morphine solutions to be injected straight into the bloodstream. Its widespread use as a painkiller in the American Civil War led to many war veterans returning home addicted to injectable morphine – 'the soldier's disease'.

CODEINE is another, milder painkiller extracted from opium. (Other common analgesics containing small amounts of narcotic include panadeine and some antihistamines.)

HEROIN, or diacetylmorphine, was extracted from morphine by the Bayer Company in 1898. (The word 'heroin' comes from the German word *heroisch*, which means heroic and powerful.) It was considered a better painkiller than morphine, as well as a highly effective cough suppressant. Physicians of the day treated opium and morphine addicts with heroin until its far worse addictive effects were recognised.

Pure heroin is a white crystalline powder with a bitter, disagreeable taste. To get the maximum effect, the orgasm-like rush of euphoria, users inject ('mainline') heroin directly into a vein. Being water-soluble, it can be mixed with liquid and swallowed. It can also be sniffed like cocaine, placed under the tongue, and smoked.

By the early 1900s, heroin had replaced opium and morphine on the streets, and the era of the junkie, the pusher and the cartels began. International black-market networks have been formed – the Triads and Mafias, who source their opium from the Golden Triangle (Burma, Thailand and Laos) and the Golden Crescent – Afghanistan, Pakistan, Iran and India. Other

I'VE BEEN SHOOTING UP HEROIN SIX TIMES A DAY FOR TWO YEARS AND I HAVEN'T FOUND IT HABIT FORMING YET...

sources include Turkey and South America.

Tragically, many people in these and other poor countries see opium and cocaine as cash crops necessary for their survival. International agencies have endeavoured without much success to encourage the planting of alternative cash crops.

Heroin and the other narcotic analgesics act by depressing the brain in a similar fashion to alcohol and barbiturates. Unlike those drugs, however, heroin also relieves pain by acting directly on the sensory areas of the thalamus and the cerebral cortex.

In larger doses it induces sleep. Lethal overdoses result from heroin's selective depressant action on the respiratory centre in the medulla.

Heroin has a rapid onset of action, beginning with a flush of euphoria and feelings of peace and contentment. It makes the user indifferent to hunger and sexual urges, and masks all inhibitions, fears and remorse – shielding the user from his or her immediate environment, both internal and external. This makes heroin one of the most addictive of all the illicit drugs. Its painkilling effect is three times that of morphine.

Unlike the barbiturates and alcohol, narcotics don't trigger aggressive behaviour. Unpleasant side effects can include vomiting, constipation, libido suppression and itching.

Because heroin lowers risk perception, users become indifferent to the dangers of using dirty needles. Skin abscesses are common. Users risk blood poisoning (septicemia), inflammation of the heart valves and lining (endocarditis), hepatitis and AIDS.

REJECTING HEROIN

Many users are known to take other substances of abuse, such as alcohol, marijuana and prescription drugs, to tide them over between fixes, or during withdrawal. Therapists can never presume they are dealing with a rational mind when deciding on appropriate detoxification techniques in withdrawal and maintenance programmes.

The symptoms of heroin withdrawal are not as severe, dangerous or lengthy as those associated with barbiturate addiction, but they are far from pleasant.

The severity depends on many factors, such as length of addiction, general state of health and whether withdrawal is forced or voluntary.

Typical symptoms of withdrawal are restlessness, lack of sleep, gooseflesh, tremors, irritability, joint and muscle pains, abdominal cramps, profuse sweating followed by chills, runny nose, nausea, vomiting, diarrhoea, urinary incontinence, shortness of breath, and

Drugs are never the answer; there are only three occasions on which I think narcotics are permitted:

involuntary muscle spasms (hence the term 'kicking the habit'). Reactions usually peak in a few days and can linger for several weeks, but the craving – what junkies themselves call the 'love affair' – can last many months.

HOW NARCOTICS WORK

The term 'narcotic' comes from a Greek word meaning to numb. The derivatives of the opium poppy are commonly called opiates. The term 'opioids' covers all substances, naturally occurring and synthetic, with opiate-like properties. Morphine and codeine are naturally occurring alkaloids. Heroin, dilaudid and meperidine are semi-synthetic substances.

Methadone was first synthesised during the Second World War by German chemists and given the brand name Dolophine in tribute to Adolf Hitler.

Also synthetic are a whole family of narcotic antagonists – laboratory-made substances that can block or counter the effects of narcotics. These drugs can be useful when someone overdoses.

Narcotics are absorbed relatively quickly from the gut when ingested. They reach the brain faster still when sniffed and absorbed through the nasal mucosa. Subcutaneous or intramuscular injections of heroin or morphine ('skin-popping') peak in the brain within 30 to 60 minutes. When smoked, heroin can reach the brain within minutes. Intravenous injections of heroin take eight to 15 seconds to reach the brain.

Heroin is rapidly converted by the liver into morphine, which is then excreted in the urine. Ninety percent of the original dose of heroin is excreted as morphine within the first 24 hours.

Heroin is also eliminated as morphine in sweat, saliva and breast milk. In pregnant women it crosses the placenta into the foetal bloodstream: paediatricians report that a growing number of such infants are born as narcotic addicts. They are treated with paregoric – a soothing tincture of opium – or

The medical profession is now well aware of the situation and is educating its young and trusting practitioners accordingly.

There is also abuse of other minor, less potent, analgesics that include over-the-counter prescriptions for pain relief, such as aspirin or paracetamol. Other analgesics which contain small amounts of narcotic are codeine, panadeine, and some antihistamines.

Over 2500 years ago, the Greeks used extracts of willow and poplar bark in the treatment of pain, gout and other illnesses. The American Indians used a tea brewed from willow bark to relieve pain. In 1838 scientists identified the active ingredient in these barks 'salicylate'. The drug known as aspirin – acetyl salicylic acid, was synthesised by the German pharmaceutical company, Bayer, and went on sale in 1915, becoming one of the most widely used drugs in the world. People abusing other drugs seldom use aspirin as prescribed. Excessive aspirin use can damage stomach lining and lead to kidney failure.

childbirth, a visit from the in-laws, and fitting into something for a fourth of July party in Nags Head.

LIBBY GELMAN-WAXNER

methadone in decreasing dosages until the withdrawal symptoms have been alleviated. Low birth weight and an increased neo-natal mortality rate follow chronic narcotic use during pregnancy.

Adolescent use of narcotics is on the increase internationally – and it's no longer strictly related to heroin supply. Thanks to 'home-bake', backyard chemists are able to make morphine from prescription codeine and panadeine. Others raid gardens for a certain variety of poppy, and milk the pods for naturally occurring narcotic alkaloids. Some do the rounds of medical centres faking severe back pain or renal colic, and are prescribed painkillers by compassionate but naïve doctors.

OPIATE STREET SLANG NAMES.

BLACK STUFF, BROWN STUFF, BIG M,

EMM, GOD'S MEDICINE, BIG BAG,

BIG H, GEAR, 'H', HAMMER, JACK,

BROWN ROCKS, CRAP, HARD STUFF,

HORSE, JUNK, POISON, SKAG, SMACK,

TEMMIES, MISTIES, MAINLINE.

Steroids

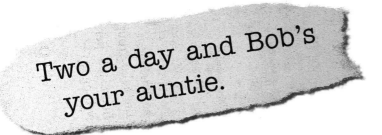

Two a day and Bob's your auntie.

Steroids are naturally occurring organic substances of great importance in biology, and their synthetic derivatives are of enormous value in medicine and chemistry. The steroid group includes all sex hormones, adrenal cortical hormones, bile acids and many other biologically active substances in animals and plants.

SOURCE: Naturally occurring in many plants, and all animals. Many synthetic derivatives now widely available.

HISTORY: Anabolic steroids – the synthetic analogue of the male hormone testosterone – were developed in the 1960s. Their use and abuse is a recent phenomenon.

NEUROTRANSMITTERS AFFECTED: Testosterone.

BRAIN SITES AFFECTED: Cortex and midbrain, particularly the hypothalamus and pituitary gland, which regulate hormone production in the body's endocrine glands.

BODY SITES AFFECTED: Gonads, endocrine glands, heart, skeletal muscle and bone.

ACUTE EFFECTS: Increased muscle size and increased explosive strength.

CHRONIC EFFECTS: Stunts vertical growth, shrinks genitals and increases breasts in men; also lowers sperm production, which can lead to sterility and increase the chances of testicular and prostate cancer. In women, causes menstrual irregularities and suppresses ovarian function. Raises blood pressure, enlarges the heart, damages the liver, suppresses the immune system, causes fluid retention in the body, heightens the risk of strokes, can cause acne that spreads from face to neck and back, and alters personality by increasing aggression, irritability and depression.

Steroid research dates from the early nineteenth century, when chemists first isolated cholesterol and some of the bile acids. In 1949, the previously untreatable symptoms of rheumatoid arthritis were dramatically alleviated by use of the adrenal hormone cortisone. A flourishing steroid pharmaceutical industry has since developed.

The synthetic steroids of therapeutic value include a number of anti-inflammatory drugs, growth-stimulating agents and oral contraceptives. Other medical uses include treating the side effects of chemotherapy, asthma, arthritis, breast cancer and many syndromes with sometimes spectacular, if inexplicable, results.

The most commonly abused steroids are the growth-stimulating hormones – the anabolic steroids, which are synthetic derivatives of the hormone testosterone. Testosterone is produced in copious amounts in the testes of men, and in far smaller but crucial amounts in the ovaries of women. Testosterone is called the 'male' hormone because it is responsible for the development of secondary sexual characteristics in adolescent males, including the growth of extra muscle and bone mass.

That's why some athletes cheat. Sportsmen and sportswomen wanting to increase their physical strength and stamina can do so chemically by ingesting huge doses of anabolic steroids. Times and performances can improve beyond what is possible through normal training, but all athletes who take performance-enhancing drugs, including amphetamines and painkillers, literally risk life and limb.

The misuse of drugs in human sport and the doping of racehorses and greyhounds has a long history, but the practice has become more widespread and sophisticated during the last 10 years, much to the alarm of international sporting and medical authorities. More disturbing still, many countries now report adolescent and teen use in high schools.

What young men have to consider is that while anabolic steroid use might take 10 seconds off their 1500 metres time, it might also take 10 millimetres off their genitals. When they enter the home straight and head for the line, 'breasting' the tape won't just be a figure of speech.

In males, anabolic steroid abuse shrinks the testicles, lowers the sperm count, and causes impotence, baldness and breast enlargement. In females, it reduces fertility, deepens the voice, increases facial and chest hair, shrinks the breasts and enlarges the clitoris.

Tragically, even athletes who stop using anabolic steroids often find that their bodies never completely return to normal.

STEROID STREET
SLANG NAMES.

CORTIES, ANDROS,
MONES, 'H', 'ROIDS.

PART 3

THE HARD SCIENCE

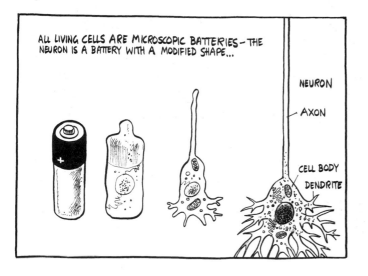

All living cells are microscopic batteries — the neuron is a battery with a modified shape...

NEURON
AXON
CELL BODY
DENDRITE

THE CELLULAR BATTERY

All living cells are batteries capable of storing an electrical charge. Surrounding every cell, much like a shell encasing a battery, is a membrane composed of a double layer of lipids (fats) and proteins that limits the flow of materials into and out of the cell. A few chemicals such as water, oxygen and carbon dioxide can move back and forth freely. For bigger molecules, movement depends on the state of special channels in the membrane wall. When the channels are open the membrane is said to be more porous, or permeable.

This permeability is strictly controlled. By deliberately pumping out certain electrically charged chemicals (mostly sodium and calcium ions) and keeping in other electrically charged chemicals (mostly potassium ions), cells are able to hold a small negative charge in their interior.

This voltage difference of minus 70 millivolts across the cell membrane is costly to maintain but it means the cell has a store of electrical energy should it need any in a hurry.

The sodium and potassium pumps keep a cell negatively charged much like a generator continually charges a car battery when the engine is running. In the morning, when huge amounts of electrical energy are needed to rotate a cold engine and fire the spark plugs, the stored voltage in the battery is large enough to provide the necessary electrical current.

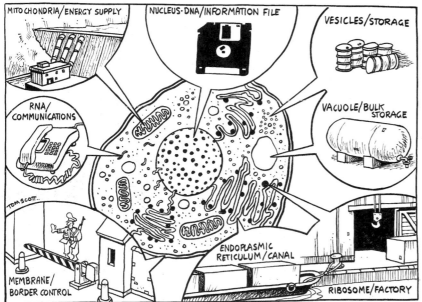

MITOCHONDRIA/ENERGY SUPPLY
NUCLEUS-DNA/INFORMATION FILE
VESICLES/STORAGE
RNA/COMMUNICATIONS
VACUOLE/BULK STORAGE
TOM SCOTT
MEMBRANE/BORDER CONTROL
ENDOPLASMIC RETICULUM/CANAL
RIBOSOME/FACTORY

NEURONS ARE SPECIAL BATTERIES

Neurons are uniquely adapted to take advantage of their stored voltage. What separates them from the billions and billions of other cellular batteries in the body is their particular shape. Most other cells are neat and compact like microscopic torch batteries. Neurons are not so tidy. They are microscopic batteries that stretch, twist and divide in hugely complicated pathways. Stored voltage is used to send electrical pulses down these pathways.

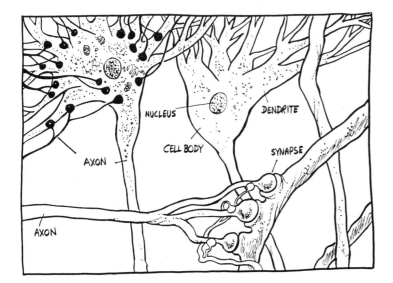

If there was such a thing as a typical neuron it would have a central section – the cell body. Sprouting from the cell body would be thousands of irregular branchlike projections – the dendrites. Extending from the other side of the cell body would be a single trunk-like projection – the axon.

Dendrites are receivers of information – input. They collect signals from other neurons and send this information to the cell body. Axons are transmitters of information – output. They send this information on to other neurons. Axons are uniform in diameter, and in vertebrates (animals with bones) they can be covered in a special insulating layer of fat-filled cells called the myelin sheath.

Within the brain, the distance electrical pulses have to travel down an axon are mostly small, only microns in some instances, but they can also be huge. In an adult giraffe, for example, axons of the motor nerves controlling the movement of the ankle in a hind leg have to journey five metres from the motor cortex in the brain, down the neck, and along the length of the spinal cord to where they eventually connect with other neurons that send their axons all the way down to the muscles at the end of the leg.

ELECTRICAL MESSAGES

The detailed biochemistry of how these currents are generated and propagated down the dendrites and axons is beyond the scope of this book. For our purposes, it is sufficient to know that some event at the tip of the dendrite interrupts the machinery controlling channels in the membrane wall. The channels open. Sodium ions flood in. A localised area of the dendrite interior which previously had more negative ions is suddenly swamped by positive ions. This change in charge is called a depolarisation.

The beauty of a localised depolarisation is that it opens up the channels in the next section of the membrane causing it to depolarise as well, and this depolarisation opens up the next section of membrane and so on. In a fraction of a second a wave of depolarisation is sent on its way to the cell body and eventually on down the axon.

Eventually is not quite the right word. Nerve impulses can travel at speeds of 10 metres a second. In axons surrounded by the insulating myelin sheaths, the velocity may reach 100 metres a second.

Axons run to the dendrites of other neurons or connect with other specialised cells like skeletal muscle. These connections, which are in fact small gaps, are termed synapses. Axon tips are typically bulb-shaped and filled with minute reservoirs called vesicles which contain the neurotransmitters.

The membrane surrounding the vesicles is similar to the presynaptic neuron membrane. When the wave of depolarisation – the electrical pulse –

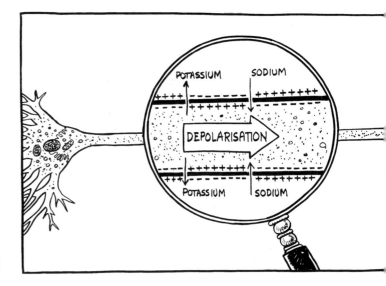

reaches the end of the axon it causes some of the vesicle's walls to fuse with the axon membrane, effectively discharging their contents into the synaptic gap. It's much like a pimple moving to the surface of the skin and bursting.

These neurochemicals attach themselves to special receptors in the postsynaptic membrane triggering a further wave of depolarisation. In the case of another neuron, the electrical message is passed on. In the case of a skeletal muscle, the depolarisation causes the muscle to contract.

NEUROTRANSMITTERS

The first neurotransmitter discovered was acetylcholine when, in 1921, the German pharmacologist Otto Loewi isolated the chemical messenger released from the axon tips of motor nerves which caused skeletal muscle to contract.

Over the next fifty years, dozens more were discovered. New ones are being discovered all the time. According to some estimates, there could be more than 2,000 neurotransmitters operating in the human brain.

MURDEROUS MICE

Nitric oxide is an important neurotransmitter in mice and men. When scientists at John Hopkins University bred special mice in which the gene essential to the synthesis of nitric oxide had been blocked, they discovered they had inadvertently created a strain of extraordinarily ferocious male rodents (females were unaffected).

Every morning when they checked the lab where their experimental animals were housed, they found one or two dead mice. At first they suspected heart attacks but on closer inspection they found tufts of fur and bloodstains confirming they had bred killer rodents. Fast and fearless, these super-aggressive mice were six times more likely to pick a fight compared with normal mice and engaged in excessive and inappropriate sexual advances, mounting females despite substantial vocal protestations.

Researchers speculate that nitric oxide may affect the emotion-regulating areas of the brain by dampening down aggressive male behaviour. Much more research is needed to establish that a nitric oxide deficiency contributes to violent impulses in humans.

NEUROTRANSMITTER TYPES

Like the people they serve, transmitters come in all shapes and sizes. Some are inhibitory – they close the channels in the postsynaptic membrane making it more negative than normal. This hyperpolarisation makes this section of the neuron less responsive to subsequent waves of depolarisation.

Other neurotransmitters are excitatory – they open the channels in the postsynaptic membrane making this section of the neuron less negative than normal. This partial depolarization makes this section of the neuron more sensitive to subsequent waves of depolarization.

It used to be thought that axons released only one kind of transmitter affecting only one type of receptor, and that synapses were simple switches that turned a postsynaptic neuron on or off. Recent work shows that synapses are more like dimmer switches.

Several kinds of transmitter can be released across a synapse and they can react with several types of their own receptor. Structurally, some transmitters are simple molecules, like the gas nitrous oxide. Some are amino acid fragments – the amines. Some are simple amino acids like gamino butyric acid (GABA), glycine, and glutamic acid. Many are small chains of amino acids linked together to form peptides, like 'Substance P', the transmitter in pain pathways. Others are made from chains of peptides linked together to form proteins.

These peptides and proteins can't be forged elsewhere in the body and delivered like crude ingots to the brain for further processing. Complex molecules have to be manufactured on the premises, in the axon tips themselves, from simpler raw materials – amino acids.

Neurotransmitters are mostly manufactured at night while we sleep, and consumed next day when we are awake. Fasting and malnutrition will limit the amount of neurotransmitters the brain can replenish; so will sleep deprivation. Sleep deprivation is the basis of brainwashing. The levels of crucial neurotransmitters go down and defiance rapidly becomes compliance. People kept awake for three days will start to hallucinate. Even broken sleep can profoundly alter moods.

All the raw materials destined for the brain have to be relatively simple molecules. Be it carbohydrates for energy or proteins for repair and maintenance, brain cells have to have their food cut up for them, otherwise none of it will get through a special protective membrane – the blood–brain barrier.

Not content with housing the brain in a vault of bone, the body has provided it with a secret last line of defence made up from pancake-like endothelial cells which wrap themselves tightly around the entire length of every single capillary in the brain. It is the cranial equivalent of the ozone layer.

The blood–brain barrier denies entry of large molecules into the brain. Small molecules such as water, oxygen, glucose, electrolytes, vitamins, and amino acids pass through easily. Unfortunately, all the mood-altering drugs are also small enough to pass through the barrier.

HOW MOOD-ALTERING DRUGS WORK

The meeting place between electricity and chemistry, the synapse, is where mood-altering drugs such as LSD, alcohol, sleeping pills, morphine, marijuana, tranquillisers and antidepressants weave their sometimes black magic.

In various ways, mood-altering drugs interfere in the orderly manufacture, the orderly release, and the orderly reabsorption or breakdown of neurotransmitters.

◆ A mood-altering substance can be any chemical that mimics the effect of a neurotransmitter by directly stimulating the receptor of the postsynaptic cell. Nicotine, for example, stimulates certain receptors in heart muscle, skeletal muscle and the cerebral cortex that normally respond to the neurotransmitter acetylcholine.

◆ A mood-altering substance can be any chemical that prematurely empties the vesicles flooding the synapse with industrial-strength quantities of the neurotransmitter. Amphetamine increases the release of noradrenalin and the user is immediately rewarded with an elevation in mood, but a few hours later a rebound state of depression follows as the brain is unable to resynthesise new noradrenalin fast enough to replace the depleted stores.

◆ A mood-altering substance can be any chemical which slows the presynaptic re-uptake of the neurotransmitters it has released, thus prolonging their effect on the postsynaptic neuron. Cocaine blocks the re-uptake of noradrenalin and dopamine. The much-hailed antidepressant Prozac blocks the re-uptake of serotonin.

◆ A mood-altering substance can be any chemical which inhibits the enzymes that normally vacuum-clean the receptor sites clear of neurotransmitters after it has done its job. The drug physostigmine blocks the enzyme that breaks down acetylcholine thus prolonging the effect of acetylcholine on the postsynaptic neuron.

◆ A mood-altering substance can be any chemical that prevents the manufacture of a neurotransmitter. The psychedelic drug PCP works by interrupting the production of serotonin.

◆ A mood-altering substance can be any chemical that has a similar structure to a transmitter and is thus able to occupy and block its receptor. Caffeine, which is similar in structure to the transmitter adenosine, works by plugging adenosine receptors. The psychedelic drug LSD is similar in structure to serotonin and works by plugging serotonin receptors.

◆ A mood-altering substance can be any chemical that can attach to one postsynaptic receptor and modify the sensitivity of a neighbouring receptor. The brain's own tranquilliser is the inhibitory neurotransmitter gamino butyric acid (GABA). The benzodiazepine tranquillisers attach themselves to receptors adjacent to GABA receptors and render them more sensitive to their own gamino butyric acid transmitter, thus intensifying the brain's own calming mechanisms.

◆ Other mood-altering drugs can act directly on the axon. Local anaesthetic drugs like Novocaine and Xylocaine attach themselves to the sodium channels in the axon membrane preventing sodium from entering the cell. Depolarisation isn't possible and no message can be sent. When local anaesthetics are applied to sensory nerves, such as nerves carrying pain messages, they stop that information reaching the brain.

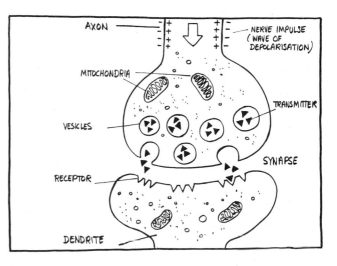

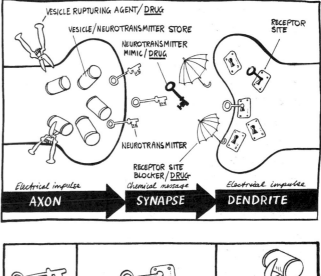

ENDORPHIN	PAIN RELIEF/ENDURANCE	HEROIN/MARIJUANA
DOPAMINE NOREPINEPHRINE	MUSCLE TONE/STIMULATION/ENERGY MOTIVATION/CONCENTRATION	NICOTINE/CAFFEINE COCAINE/AMPHETAMINE
SEROTONIN	MENTAL STABILITY/SLEEP CONTROL APPETITE/SELF ESTEEM	ALCOHOL/NICOTINE COCAINE/PCP
GAMMA AMINO BUTYRIC ACID	MUSCLE RELAXANT/TRANQUILLIZER	ALCOHOL/NICOTINE MARIJUANA
ACETYLCHOLINE	MEMORY/LEARNING	MARIJUANA/NICOTINE
CORTISONE CORTICOTROPIN	IMMUNE SYSTEM/HEALING STRESS	HEROIN/ANABOLIC STEROIDS/COCAINE

USEFUL ORGANISATIONS

ADFAM National
32–36 Loman Street
London SE1 0EE
Tel: 0171 928 8900
Help and advice for the families and friends of drug users.

Alcohol Concern
32–36 Loman Street
London SE1 0EE
Tel: 0171 928 7377
Information on alcohol use and abuse.

Health Education Authority
Tel: 0171 413 2030
Information about their drugs and solvents initiatives.

Institute for the Study of Drug Dependence
32–36 Loman Street
London SE1 0EE
Tel: 0171 928 1211
The ISDD is an independent charity dedicated to advancing knowledge, understanding and policy-making about drugs. The Institute produces the pamphlets D-Word (for parents) and D-Brief (for teenagers) which provide basic information on drugs, and they also publish the magazine D-mag – this aims to answer many of the questions young people ask about drugs.

Life Education Centres
First Floor
53–56 Great Sutton Street
London EC1V 0DE
Tel: 0171 490 3210
Life Education Centres is a national charity that inspires children with the knowledge, skills and self-confidence to make healthy choices for their future, in particular the avoidance of drug use. For books, information packs, videos, multimedia packages and mobile learning centres, contact the above address.

National Drugs Helpline
Tel: 0800 776600
Free, confidential advice and information (including lists of local UK agencies) 24 hours a day.

Re-Solv
30a High Street
Stone
Staffordshire ST15 8JP
Tel: 01785 817885
Information and advice about solvents.

GLOSSARY

acetaldehyde a poisonous substance: breakdown product of ethyl alcohol.

acetylcholine a neurotransmitter.

acute of sudden onset and brief duration.

addiction constant craving for and dependency on a drug.

adenosine a neurotransmitter.

adrenalin a hormone released from the adrenal gland, also a neurotransmitter.

adrenocortical hormones hormones released from the adrenal cortex.

Alzheimer's disease a disease of old age, marked by gradual loss of memory and psychological abilities.

amnesia loss of memory.

amphetamine a drug that stimulates the release of noradrenalin and dopamine.

analgesia relief from pain.

anaesthetic blocking all sensations from an area of the body.

antagonist (drug) a drug that blocks the effect of a synaptic transmitter or of another drug.

anterior pituitary an endocrine gland located at the base of the brain that releases hormones into the bloodstream.

attention deficit disorder a childhood condition characterised by restlessness and distractability

atropine a drug that blocks acetylcholine receptors.

axon a long fibre carrying impulses away from the cell body of a neuron towards other cells.

barbiturates a class of drugs used as anticonvulsants, sedatives and tranquillisers.

benzodiazepines a class of drugs used as tranquillisers.

blood–brain barrier a mechanism that prevents some chemicals from passing between the bloodstream and the brain.

caffeine a stimulant drug that releases the neurotransmitters adrenalin and dopamine, and interferes with adenosine.

carcinogen a cancer-causing agent.

central nervous system (CNS) the brain and the spinal cord.

cerebellum a large, highly convoluted structure in the hindbrain.

cerebral cortex the outer layer of mammalian forebrain.

chromosome a strand of DNA bearing the genes.

chronic of gradual onset and long duration.

cocaine a stimulant drug that releases noradrenalin, adrenalin and dopamine.

comatose being in a state of unconsciousness from which one cannot be aroused, even by strong stimulation.

compulsion a forced, driven behaviour.

congenital present from birth.

consolidation gradual establish-ment or strengthening of a memory.

cyclic AMP a second messenger that acts within a cell in response to a synaptic transmitter or hormone.

delusion a false, unfounded belief.

dendrite the widely branching fibres that convey information towards the cell body of a neuron.

depolarisation a reduction in the electrical gradient across a membrane.

diazepam a benzodiazepine tranquilliser (trade name: Valium).

DNA deoxyribonucleic acid, the chemical that composes the chromosomes.

dopamine a neurotransmitter, also released by the hypothalamus as a hormone.

endocrine gland a gland that releases hormones.

endoplasmic reticulum a network of thin tubes within a cell.

endorphins a category of chemicals produced by the body that have effects similar to those of opiate drugs.

enzyme any protein that catalyses biological reactions.

forebrain the most anterior (front) part of the brain, including the cerebral cortex and other structures.

GABA gamma-amino-butyric acid.

gene a physical particle that determines some aspect of inheritance.

glia supportive cells in the brain that do not transmit synaptic information.

glucocorticoids hormones released from the adrenal glands.

glucose the most common sugar in the blood, and the main fuel of neurons.

glutamate an amino acid found throughout the body, also a neurotransmitter.

glycine an amino acid found throughout the body, also a neurotransmitter.

half-life the time for half the drug to have left the body.

hallucination a sensory experience that does not correspond to external events.

hallucinogen a drug that induces hallucinations.

heroin a drug that stimulates the receptors that normally respond to endorphins.

hippocampus a large forebrain structure between the thalamus and cortex.

hormone a chemical released from an endocrine into the blood that affects other parts of the body.

hypothalamus a forebrain structure near the thalamus.

Korsakoff's syndrome a condition including memory deficits and other disorders caused by thiamine deficiency, usually secondary to chronic alcoholism.

lecithin a dietary precursor to acetylcholine.

lipids fat molecules.

long-term memory memory that continues to be stored after attention is distracted from the memory-causing event.

LSD lysergic acid diethylamide, an hallucinogenic chemical that blocks serotonin synapses for about four hours and reduces the number of serotonin receptors for days; also affects dopamine synapses.

membrane the covering that surrounds a cell.

methadone a drug given to opiate addicts as a less disabling substitute for morphine or heroin; stimulates the receptors that normally respond to endorphins.

mitochondria structures within cells that produce energy from sugars.

morphine a drug that stimulates the receptors that normally respond to endorphins.

motor cortex the part of the cerebral cortex that controls movement.

myelin sheath a fatty substance that surrounds and insulates axons.

narcolepsy a condition characterised by sudden attacks of sleep.

neuron the basic cell of the nervous system.

neurotransmitter a chemical messenger released across a synapse.

nicotine a drug that stimulates certain acetylcholine receptors.

norepinephrine aka noradrenalin, a neurotransmitter, also released by the adrenal gland as a hormone.

Novocaine an anaesthetic drug that acts by blocking the transport of sodium through the membrane.

opiates drugs derived from the seeds of opium poppies.

Parkinson's disease a disease caused by gradual destruction of the substantia nigra in the brain, an area normally rich in dopamine, resulting in loss of voluntary movement.

peptide a compound of two or more amino acids.

Pet scan positron-emission tomography, a method of mapping activity in a living brain by recording the emission of radioactivity from injected chemicals.

phyostigmine a drug used in therapy and anaesthesia. It antagonises the enzyme that breaks down acetylcholine.

pituitary gland an endocrine gland whose secretions regulate the activity of many other hormonal glands.

polarised having an electrical

gradient across a membrane.

postsynaptic cell the cell on the receiving end of a synapse.

postsynaptic membrane a specialised area of the membrane of a postsynaptic cell that is responsive to the synaptic neurotransmitter.

presynaptic cell a neuron on the releasing end of a cell.

presynaptic ending a bulge at the end of an axon from which a synaptic neurotransmitter is released.

presynaptic inhibition an effect on a presynaptic neuron that decreases its tendency to release its neurotransmitter.

presynaptic receptor a receptor on a presynaptic ending, sensitive to a synaptic neurotransmitter.

puberty (maturation) the onset of sexual maturity.

resting potential the electrical potential across a membrane when a neuron is at rest.

ribosomes structures within a cell where proteins are synthesised.

RNA ribonucleic acid, a chemical whose structure is determined by DNA, and which in turn determines the structure of proteins.

schizophrenia a mental illness characterised by mental deterioration and thought disorder and/or hallucinations or delusions.

second messenger a chemical within a neuron, activated by a synaptic transmitter, that in turn initiates processes within the neuron.

sedative something that reduces activity and excitement.

semipermeable membrane a membrane that permits only water and a few other molecules to cross.

sensitisation an increase in response to stimuli because of previous exposure to one or more intense stimuli.

sensory neuron a neuron that responds directly to a stimulus such as light, sound, or chemicals in the environment.

serotonin (5-HT) a synaptic transmitter.

short-term memory memory for an event that has just occurred.

skeletal muscle the kind of muscle found in the limbs.

spinal cord the part of the central nervous system found within the spinal column.

steroid hormones hormones derived from cholesterol that exert their effects by attaching to the chromosomes and influencing expression of the genes.

stroke an interruption of blood flow to part of the brain.

stupor partial unconsciousness or unresponsiveness.

synapse the point of communication between two neurons or between a neuron and a muscle.

synaptic block cessation of firing of a postsynaptic cell due to an excess of synaptic transmitters at a synapse.

synaptic cleft the space separating presynaptic from postsynaptic cell.

synaptic transmitter a chemical released by a neuron at a synapse that affects the activity of a second cell.

testosterone a hormone released by the gonads, more in the male than in the female.

thalamus a structure in the centre of the forebrain.

thiamine vitamin B, required for the metabolism of glucose.

tranquillisers drugs that decrease anxiety.

tricyclic drugs a group of drugs that block re-uptake of norepinephrine, dopamine and serotonin by the presynaptic neuron, often used for the treatment of depression.

tryptophan an amino acid, a precursor of serotonin.

tyrosine an amino acid that serves as the precursor to several synaptic transmitters.

Valium a benzodiazepine tranquilliser (chemical name: diazepam).

vascular pertaining to the blood vessels.

vesicle small hollow structure used for storage inside cells.

X chromosome a chromosome of which female mammals have two and males one.

Xylocaine an anaesthetic drug that acts by blocking the transport of sodium across the membrane.

Y chromosome a chromosome of which female mammals have none and males one.

ABOUT THE LIFE EDUCATION TRUST

The Life Education Trust was begun by Ted Noffs, who for 20 years ran the Wayside Chapel in Sydney's King's Cross, which tended to many big-city victims and social outcasts. The Trust now operates in a growing number of countries, including New Zealand, and has been endorsed by the United Nations as a health education initiative.

In keeping with Ted Noffs' view that prevention is far better than cure, the Trust's philosophy is to engender every child with a sense of their own worth, and to teach them that they are utterly unique, that their body systems are both miraculous and vulnerable, and that respect for themselves and others is the key to happy survival in a complex world.

The Authors would like to thank all the numerous individuals, institutions and companies that have helped to produce this book who are not specifically acknowledged.

abscesses 102
acetaldehyde 69–70, 71
acetylcholine 18, 31, 85, 92, 98, 99, 109, 110, 111
acne 104
addiction 38, 75, 78, 80, 82, 90, 92, 98, 100, 102
adenosine 111
adolescence 13–14
the adolescent brain 27–8
    boundaries, need for 48
    physiology of 13, 14
    stress 14
adrenalin 72, 79, 82
adults and substance abuse 65
ageing 97, 99
aggressive behaviour 104, 109
    see also violence
AIDS 100, 102
alcohol 32, 61, 68 71, 91, 102, 110
    and barbiturates 77
    and marijuana 39, 70
Alzheimer's disease 34, 97
amino acids 30, 31, 109–10
amphetamines 72–3, 77, 82, 105, 110
anabolic steroids 104, 105
anaemia 60
anaesthesia, uncontrolled 39, 70, 91
analgesics 78, 79, 100, 101, 102, 103, 105
anandamide 94
angel dust see PCP
antidepressants 110, 111
antihistamines 101, 103
anxiety states 38, 74, 78, 79, 80, 89, 92
appetite, changes in 16, 38, 87, 91
aspirin 103
athletes 73, 105
Ativan 77
Attention Deficit Disorder (ADD) 73

babies and children, effects of substance abuse on 38, 71, 73, 75, 82, 92, 96–7, 99, 103
barbitone 75
barbiturates 74–7
behavioural changes 16
benzodiazepines 74, 77, 111
birth defects 38, 75, 92
blame, transferring 47
blood poisoning 102
blood pressure, raised 79, 80, 82, 87, 89, 104
botanical hallucinogens 85
brain 18–19, 25–8, 62
    the adolescent brain 27–8
    the adult brain 26
    alcohol, effects of 68, 70
    axons 26, 29, 108, 109, 111
    barbiturates, effects of 74
    brain function 25–8
    cerebellum 93, 95
    cocaine, effects of 82
    electrical impulses 25, 27, 28, 107, 108–9
    endothelial cells 110
    frontal cortex 93, 95
    glial cells 25
    hippocampus 33, 34, 36, 39, 41, 93, 95, 97
    inhalants, effects of 90
    LSD, effects of 87
    marijuana, effects of 37, 39, 41, 93–5
    mood-altering chemicals in the 29–30
    mood-altering drugs, effects of 30, 31, 34, 36, 110–11
    neurons 25, 26, 27, 33, 54, 70, 107–8, 109, 111
    opiates/narcotics, effects of 100, 102
    steroids, effects of 104
    synapses 26, 29, 33, 95, 108, 109, 110

brain atrophy 41
breath, foul 91
breathlessness 79
burns on hands and clothing 16

caffeine 31, 61, 78–9, 81, 111
cancer 38, 91, 92, 97, 98, 99, 104
cannabis see hash oil; hashish; marijuana; THC
Cannabis sativa 37, 39, 92, 93
case histories 21–4, 43–6, 57–9, 63–4
cellular batteries 107
central nervous system disorders 29
cigarettes 99
circulatory disorders 80, 98, 99
cirrhosis of the liver 70
cocaine 32, 72, 80–3, 111
codeine 100, 101, 102, 103
colds and infections 16
coma 39, 70, 77, 91
concentration, impaired 17, 38, 92
confusion 71, 72, 89
constipation 102
convulsions 87
counselling 44, 45, 63
crack 82

'date-rape drug' 77
dehydration 89
demerol 100
dendrites 108
denial 15
depolarisation 108, 109, 111
depression 29, 60, 73, 79, 80, 89, 104
designer drugs 88–9
diabetes 80
diet and nutrition 31, 50, 52, 60, 61
'diet pills' 73, 78
dilaudid 102
disrespect and defiance 16, 21, 63
DMT 86

doctors 50, 60, 103
DOM 86
dopamine 72, 79, 82, 111
drug education 47–8, 49, 50
drug-free, staying 52–3
drug paraphernalia 17
drug patches 24
drug treatment agencies 50, 52

ecstasy 86, 88–9
educational underachievement 38, 92
emotional outbursts 17
endorphins 30, 92, 100
epilepsy 80
ethanol 69, 70, 71
exercise and sport 30, 50, 52–3, 61, 64
experimentation 15, 43, 49, 63, 77
eyes and nose, runny 16, 91
eyes, red 38

fasting and malnutrition 30, 110
fatigue 73, 87, 89
fertility, impaired 105
flashbacks 84, 87
fluid intake 53, 61
foetal alcohol syndrome 71

GABA (gamma amino butyric acid) 68, 75, 79, 90, 92, 98, 109–10, 111
gastric disorders 79
glue 91
growth impairment 96, 104

hallucinations 38, 84, 85, 87, 110
hallucinogens 84–9
hangovers 69
hash oil 39, 93
hashish 39, 93
headaches 79, 84, 87
heart disease 79, 80, 98, 99, 102
heartburn 78
hepatitis 100, 102
heroin 32, 100, 101–2, 103
hormones 14, 38, 92, 104

immune system, impaired 38, 61,
92, 99, 104
impotence 105
inhalants 90–1
insensitivity to others 17
insomnia 79
intellectual impairment 36, 37, 38, 39, 92

kicking drugs 60–1
Korsakoff's syndrome 71

language of substance abuse 32
laughing gas 90
leukaemia 38, 92, 97
libido 31–2, 38, 102
Librium 77
'love drug' 89
LSD 32, 86–7, 88, 110, 111
lying, habitual 15, 16, 21, 44

'magic mushrooms' 84, 85
manipulative behaviour 16, 59
marijuana 32, 37–41, 92–7, 99, 102, 110
   absorption 39, 93
   and alcohol 39, 70
   as a medicine 41
   defence of 9–10, 41
   potency 39
   side effects 37, 38, 92, 95–7
   THC concentration 39
   usage 39
Marinol 41
maturation 11, 14, 26, 27, 54
MDA 86, 89
MDMA see ecstasy
memory 33–6, 93
memory impairment and loss 17, 18, 33, 34, 36, 38, 39, 71, 92, 95
menstrual irregularities 104
mental and emotional changes 17
meperidine 102
metabolic efficiency, impaired 10–11, 39, 93
methadone 24, 100, 102, 103
miscarriage 82, 87, 99
Mogodon 77
mood-altering substances 11, 30, 31, 34, 36, 110–11

mood swings 17, 21
morphine 100, 101, 102, 103, 110

narcotics see opiates/narcotics
nausea 87, 89, 90
neurotransmitters 27, 29, 30, 31, 32, 69, 94, 108, 109–10, 111
nicotine 98–9, 110
nitric oxide 109
noradrenalin 30, 72, 79, 82, 85, 110, 111
nosebleeds 91
Notec 77
Novocaine 111

occupational performance, decline in 38, 92, 95
oestrogen 14
opiates/narcotics 30, 100–3
opium 30, 100, 101, 102
ovulation, impaired 38, 92

painkillers see analgesics
panadeine 101, 103
paracetamol 103
paranoia 38, 73, 92
paregoric 103
parents
   blaming 47
   drug education, providing 47–8
   minimising the risks for your child 49–50, 52–3
   parent power 50
   parental reactions 47, 50
   'tough love' 21, 50
Parkinson's disease 29
PCP 86, 111
pentobarbitone 75
pep pills see amphetamines
petrol 91
peyote cactus 85
phenobarbitone 75
physical changes 16
physostigmine 111
pituitary gland 14
police intervention 50
pregnancy and substance abuse 38, 39, 71, 73, 75, 79, 82, 87, 92, 93, 96–7, 99, 103

prescription drugs 24, 102
progesterone 14
Prozac 111
psychedelic experience *see* hallucinogens
psychomotor impairment 38, 92, 95
psychosis 38, 72, 80, 84, 87, 89, 92
puberty *see* maturation

reality
   altered perception of 34, 36, 87
   loss of contact with 34, 85, 87
rebellion and non-conformity 43, 48
relaxation and deep-breathing exercises 53, 61
respiratory diseases 38, 80, 92, 97, 98, 99
Ritalin 73
road accidents, substance abuse and 95
Rohypnol 77

'safe' drugs 50
saying 'no' to drugs 55
schizophrenia 29, 38, 84, 87, 92, 96
school-related changes 16, 63
secobarbitone 75
secretive behaviour 16
sedative hypnotics *see* barbiturates
self-preservation instinct 18
sensitivity, exaggerated 17
Serepax 77
serotonin 31, 85, 89, 92, 98, 111
shoplifting and stealing 16
signs of substance abuse 15–19
   behavioural changes 16
   drug paraphernalia 17
   mental and emotional changes 17
   physical changes 16
   school-related changes 16
   social changes 17
   testing for 17–18
sinsemilla 39
sleep 53, 61
sleep deprivation 30, 31, 110
sleeping habits, altered 16
sleeping pills 34, 61, 75, 110

slurred speech 16
sodium pentothal 75
solvents 32, 60, 91
sperm production, impaired 38, 39, 92, 105
steroids 104–5
stimulants 31, 61, 78–9
stomach ulcers 99
stress 14, 31
strokes 72, 80, 104
suicidal tendencies 87, 89
support groups 61

testosterone 14, 31, 39, 70, 105
THC (Delta-9 tetrahydrocannabinol) 38, 39, 41, 92, 97
   concentration 39, 93
   receptor distribution 95
thiopentone 75
throat dryness 38
time sense, distorted 17
toxicology tests 60
toxin elimination 61
tranquillisers 110, 111
truancy 16
trust 15

Valium 74, 77
violence 16, 31, 60, 70
vision, blurred 87, 89
vitamin deficiencies 71, 99
vitamin supplements 53, 61
vomiting 102
vomiting centre, inactivated 70

weight changes 16
withdrawal symptoms 61, 75, 77, 102

Xylocaine 111

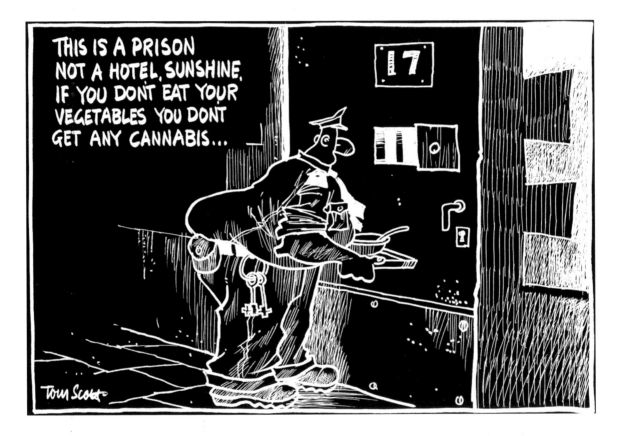